Un, deux, trois!

Upper Juniors

Years 5-6

Eileen Jones

Hopscotch

A division of MA Education Ltd

Hopscotch

A division of MA Education Ltd

Published by
Hopscotch, a division of MA
Education,
St Jude's Church, Dulwich Road,
London, SE24 0PB
www.hopscotchbooks.com
020 7738 5454

©2010 MA Education Ltd.

Written by Eileen Jones

Illustrated by Emma Turner,
Fonthill Creative, 01722 717057

ISBN 978 1 90539 081 6

Contents

Introduction

About the book

Un, deux, trois! aims to make French practical and achievable. Its exciting and appropriate material will ensure that children of all levels of ability have the opportunities to both enjoy and achieve in their language learning. And it will support you, whatever your level of linguistic confidence or competence.

This book builds on the teaching of Book 1. It continues to address three fundamental strands of language teaching: oracy, literacy and intercultural understanding. It responds to the recommendations of the National Curriculum for Foreign Languages by providing opportunities for the children to:

- become increasingly familiar with the sounds and written form of French;

- make comparisons between French and other languages;

- expand their cultural awareness;

- grow in confidence as they understand what they hear and read;

- learn to communicate;

- develop linguistic competence;

- present ideas orally to a range of audiences;

- describe people, places, things and actions orally and in writing;

- understand basic grammar appropriate to the language being studied.

Using the book

Reflecting the structure of the National Curriculum for Foreign Languages, the book is divided into twelve Units.

Each Unit forms the basis of half a term's work and covers a theme that both crosses cultures and is relevant to the children's lives. For each Unit, there is an introduction stating the main teaching points, grammar, language sounds, and vocabulary to be addressed. There are four easy-to-follow, fully planned and resourced, ready-to-use lessons. These are supported by photocopiables and follow-up ideas. Each lesson plan explains what you will need, how to prepare, what to say to the children and what to encourage them to say.

Make one lesson the core of a week's teaching. Keep returning to the contents of a lesson during the week, playing, repeating and adapting games, so you give all the children the confidence to contribute. Use the Follow-up activity as a tool for differentiation, as only more able children wil be able to complete the full task. Teach the lessons in chronological order, so learning in one lesson is a foundation for the next. Finally, draw the Unit together with the 'More ideas' section of school and home activities, using the section to revise and consolidate the lessons' main teaching points and extend opportunities to learn about French culture.

The main aim of language teaching is to develop linguistic competence, so be ready to adapt material to suit your opportunities. A game used in one Unit may be easily adapted to consolidate learning in another Unit. Similarly, grasp opportunities to take French beyond timetabled lessons and into other areas of classroom life. Most of all, generate enthusiasm, as children gain pleasure from their language-learning skills.

France is in the continent of Europe

FRANCE

Un, deux, trois!

Unit 13 Bon appétit!

(Enjoy your meal!)

Unit theme
- Food and drink

Teaching points
- Talking about what has been eaten and drunk
- Making simple statements about food and drink
- Expressing likes, dislikes and preferences about food and drink
- Understanding and giving instructions
- Following and writing recipes

Grammar
- Perfect tense: *manger (j'ai mangé, tu as mangé); boire (j'ai bu)*
- *les* and *des* with plural nouns
- compound sentences containing *et* and *mais*
- Agreement of adjectives: masculine and feminine plural
- Imperatives: *vous* form of regular and irregular verbs
- Using *du, de la, de l', des*

Language sounds
- *on/onne*
- *an/en*
- *au/eau*

Vocabulary

Dans le sac il y a...	In the bag there is …
J'ai mangé	I ate
J'ai bu	I drank
Tu as mangé (une banane)?	Did you eat (a banana)?
et	and
mais	but

Il est bon/mauvais (pour la santé)	It is good/bad (for your health) (masculine singular)
Elle est bonne/mauvaise (pour la santé)	Is good/bad (to your health) (feminine singular)
Ils sont bons/mauvais (pour la santé)	They are good/bad (for your health) (masculine plural)
Elles sont bonnes/ mauvaises (pour la santé)	They are good/bad (for your health) (feminine plural)
Il te faut...	You need...
un sandwich au fromage/ jambon/chocolat/thon	a cheese/ ham/ chocolate/ tuna sandwich
un gâteau	a cake
une banane	a banana
une pomme	an apple
une orange	an orange
des chips	some crisps
du fromage	some cheese
de l'eau	some water
Comme casse-croûte j'ai ...	In my packed lunch, I have…
le caramel	toffee
le chocolat	chocolate
le chocolat chaud	hot chocolate
la soupe	soup
les pommes de terre au four	baked potatoes
les saucisses	sausages
du pain pita	some pitta bread
de la sauce tomate	some tomato sauce
des tomates	some tomatoes
des champignons	some mushrooms
du fromage râpé	some grated cheese
de la sauce caramel	toffee sauce
des bonbons	some sweets

Instructions are given in the polite (plural) form

Mettez	Put
Mettez ... sur	Put ... on
Faites	Make
Coupez en tranches	Slice

Ajoutez	Add	*Qu'est-ce que tu as comme goûter?*	What have you got as a snack?
Mélangez	Mix		
Mélangez avec ...	Mix with...	*Tu as (une banane)?*	Have you got (a banana)?
Versez	Pour		
Laissez cuire	Leave to cook	*Tu aimes (les bananes)?*	Do you like (bananas)?
Faites sauter	Flip	*Tu as bu (de l'eau)?*	Did you drink (water)?
Chauffez la pizza au four	Heat the pizza in the oven	*Combien d'enfants préfèrent les sandwichs au...?*	How many children prefer ... sandwiches?
Prêt(e)	Ready	*Qu'est-ce qu'il y a dans le sac?*	What's in the bag?

Additional vocabulary for teachers

Qu'est-ce que tu as comme casse-croûte?	What have you got as a packed lunch?

Resources
Food and food pictures

Lesson 1 Mon casse-croûte (My packed lunch)

Resources
Food pictures or props; six lunch boxes; a feely bag of plastic (or real) fruit and vegetables; one copy of photocopiable 6A, Book 1

- Display the food pictures from photocopiable 6A, Unit 6, Book 1. How many names can partners tell each other? Share results, turning over the pictures to check.

- Say and write new foods: *une banane, un sandwich, du fromage, de l'eau, des chips, une orange, un gâteau, le jus d'orange,* the children repeating them after you.

- Select a list of 8-10 appropriate packed lunch foods to leave on the whiteboard. Give everyone a piece of card to choose and write one of them for their lunch.

- Arrange the children in a large circle and play **La salade mixte** (mixed salad):
  - Call out a food name: those children change places.
  - Call out two food names: those children can change places.
  - Call out *La salade mixte*: anyone can change places with someone.
  - After two or three minutes of playing, check how mixed your salad is!

- Put the children into groups of four to six to share food information as they question one another:
  - *Qu'est-ce que tu as comme casse-croûte? (J'ai...)*

- Ask everyone to mime eating a food. Ask *Qu'est-ce que tu manges ?* (What are you eating?) In reply, a child should say *Je mange un sandwich.* (I am eating a sandwich).

- Ask the children to draw something they ate yesterday. Ask *Qu'est-ce que tu mangé hier? (What did you eat yesterday?)* In reply, a child should say *J'ai mangé... un sandwich.* (I ate a... sandwich.)

- Explain that *J'ai mangé* and *J'ai bu* (I drank) are past tense forms of verbs, used when talking about things that have already happened. Practise them as a whole class.

- Give each group a lunch-box and explain **Carry-on!**
  - One group member puts his food in the lunch box and says *Comme casse-croûte j'ai* (+ the name of his food). The box passes to the next person who, having added her food to the box, repeats what the first person said and the name of her food. So the box gets fuller and the chant gets longer. (Children may find it easier to speak as a group, individuals only saying alone their food name.)
  - Listen to every group's packed-lunch box. Vote on which sounds tastiest.

- Finish by playing **Feel around**. Give partners a 10 second feel of your prepared feely bag of plastic fruit and vegetables. Ask *Qu'est-ce qu'il y a dans le sac?* The class replies *Dans le sac il y a...* and partners say one food they think they have identified. After every pair has had a turn, how many of your secret foods have the children discovered?

Follow-up
Suggest making a packed-lunch timetable, the children drawing and labelling their planned packed-lunches for the school week.

Un, deux, trois!

Lesson 2
C'est bon pour la santé?
(Is it good for your health?)

Resources
Food pictures or props from Lesson 1;
photocopiable 13A

- Revise and introduce food vocabulary by showing pictures or props.

- Bring out a container labelled *Bon pour la santé*. Confirm the meaning.

- Ask the children to help you identify healthy foods. Agree on a healthy sign (for example, a thumbs up). Say only <u>singular masculine</u> foods, for example: *le gâteau, le fromage, le caramel, un sandwich au jambon, le cresson* (cress). When the children make the agreed sign, help them say their verdict in a sentence, for example: *Un sandwich au jambon est bon pour la santé. Le gâteau n'est pas bon pour la santé.*

- Use a singular feminine noun in the same sentence construction. For example: *Une pomme est bonne pour la santé*. Display the written sentences. Can the children spot an important spelling difference? (*bon* has become *bonne*) Confirm the feminine agreement between the noun and the adjective.

- Announce a hearing test! Give everyone two hearing cards, *bon* and *bonne*. (Some children may prefer to work with a partner, one card each). Read out assorted masculine and feminine sentences, for example: *Le chocolat n'est pas bon pour la santé. Une banana est bonne pour la santé.* Stop after each for the children to hold up a card. Confirm if they are correct. After 10 sentences, how many hearing points did they get? Does their hearing need a re-test?

- Give further practice in adjective agreement by repeating the previous teaching activities for the adjective forms *mauvais* and *mauvaise*.

- Remind the children about the conjunctions *et* and *mais*. Demonstrate their use to form a longer, compound sentence from two short sentences: *J'aime le fromage <u>et</u> le fromage est bon pour la santé. J'aime le caramel <u>mais</u> le caramel n'est pas bon pour la santé. J'aime les tomates <u>mais</u> je préfère les bananes.*

- Divide the class into three groups **A, B** and **C**. Set these tasks:
  - **Group A**: children write a short sentence beginning *J'aime…* and complete it with a food.
  - **Group B**: children write a short food sentence beginning *Il est…* or *Elle est…* and complete it

with a comment about whether it is healthy.
  - **Group C**: children work with a partner, making and writing two conjunction cards, *et* and *mais*.

- Ask **A** children to find a **B** sentence that matches their noun, the new partners then searching for the **C** conjunction they think will suit them. (Have a supply of spare **B** sentences and **C** conjunctions.)

- Challenge each new **A B C** group to join up into a compound sentence, standing in order as they say their sentence to the class. Does the class agree with the choice of conjunction?

Follow-up
Give the children photocopiable 13A to complete, reminding them of the use of the pronouns *il/elle/ ils/elles* to replace nouns and the need for adjectives and nouns or pronouns to agree.

Lesson 3 14 juillet (July 14)

Resources
Access to the Internet

- Make sure the days of the week and months of the year are on prominent display.

- Put the children into teams of three to play **Make a date**. Allocate roles: one person the day, one the date, the third person the month.

- Call out a date, for example *lundi 7 octobre*, for team members to write their part on their individual whiteboard and quickly stand in the correct order. Award team points to the correct human dates made in the time allowed.

- As the children improve, reduce the time allowed or award points to only the first three correct teams.

- Warn the children that for your final date they need only two roles. Call out *14 juillet*.

- Write the last date on the whiteboard. Do the children know its significance in France? Explain:
  - it marks an event in history;
  - it is Bastille Day;
  - Bastille Day is an annual celebration in France;
  - it is a national holiday;
  - there are big celebrations everywhere: parades, holiday food, bonfires and fireworks.

- Ask the children which English celebration sounds similar? Why? Point out that Bonfire Night also marks an event in history and has bonfires and fireworks to celebrate the occasion.

- Emphasise the importance of food in celebrations. Let the children work with a partner to list in French six fun foods that will suit an evening bonfire and fireworks party for either Bonfire Night or Bastille Day.

Follow-up

Ask the children to make a poster advertising a bonfire celebration, drawing and labelling (in French) the food that will be available. Suggest putting an English flag on one half of the poster and a French flag on the other to emphasise the link between the two countries' celebrations.

Lesson 4
Le Croque-Monsieur
(Croque-Monsieur)

Resources

Food pictures or props; individual copies of photocopiable 13B

● Remind the children about Bastille Day (Lesson 3), its celebrations and the importance of food. It is in July and a French national holiday, so picnics are popular.

● Have the children heard of a *Croque-Monsieur*? (A popular French toasted cheese and ham sandwich).

● Display pictures and say: *Ingrédients: du pain, du fromage râpé, du jambon.* (The ingredients: bread, grated cheese, ham). Read out your recipe, using action and mime to clarify meanings: *Méthode*
- **Coupez** *deux tranches du pain.*
- **Mettez** *le fromage sur le pain.*
- **Ajoutez** *du jambon.*
- **Faites** *un sandwich.*
- **Chauffez** *le sandwich au four.*
- **Voilà** *un Croque-Monsieur!*

● Repeat the instructions, this time the children miming the actions.
Write the ingredients, recipe and two headings (*Ingrédients, Méthode*) on the whiteboard. Can the children identify the verbs highlighted in the recipe? Point out their position at the start of sentences and their role of giving commands. Guide the children to identifying them as imperatives.

● Pretend it is Bastille Day! Give the children permission to create their own *Croque-Monsieur*. With sweet or savoury ingredients, the sandwich does not have to be healthy!

● Let the children plan their ideas, using bilingual dictionaries to list their ingredients.

Follow-up

Give the children photocopiable 13B to complete, suggesting they first write their recipe in rough. Encourage helpful illustrations and inventive sandwich names. Afterwards, use the recipes to compile a class cookery book.

Celebrations for Bastille Day begin the night before, all over the country, but the best firework displays are in Paris.

Un, deux, trois!

Bon appétit!

adjectives	adjectives	conjunctions
bon	mauvais	et
bonne	mauvaise	mais
bons	mauvaises	
bonnes		

Part 1

For sentences labelled **a**, fill the gap with the correct food noun.

For sentences labelled **b**, choose the adjective to agree with the noun.

1 a J'aime une – _____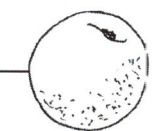
 b Elle est... pour la santé.

2 a J'aime le – _____
 b Il est... pour la santé.

3 a J'aime le – _____
 b Il est... pour la santé.

4 a Je n'aime pas le – _____
 b Il est... pour la santé.

5 a J'aime les – _____
 b Ils sont... pour la santé.

6 a Je n'aime pas les – _____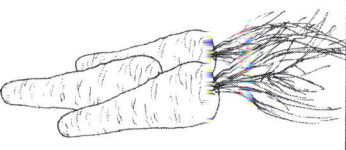
 b Elles sont... pour la santé.

Part 2
Make one sentence from each pair of sentences, using the conjunction
et or **mais**.

_____

Ingrédients

Méthode

More ideas for...

Work at school

- Make **Carry-on!** (Lesson 1) into a regular favourite by organising quick games. This will extend the children's food vocabulary and improve their confidence as speakers.

- Suggest the children make a bilingual food dictionary. Encourage them to think carefully about how to organise it for easy reference. Will illustrations help? Will computer presentation make it easier to add new words? What about alphabetical order?

- Use the data collected in the **Follow-up** activity to Lesson 1 for the children, with the help of a partner, to award between one and five '*Bonne santé*' (Healthy eating) stars to each of their lunches. Suggest the children total their stars. Use an ICT lesson for the children to present the data in graphical representation (they could combine information with a partner.) Afterwards ask them to interpret the graphs. What facts are shown about their eating habits? Is one day particularly likely to be unhealthy?

- Let the children make and taste a classic *Croque-Monsieur* by following the recipe in Lesson 4. Put the children into small groups and provide the ingredients to make a sandwich. Use a sandwich-maker to toast each sandwich. Afterwards ask the children to write about their reactions. Provide sentence ideas, for example:

  J'aime /Je n'aime pas le Croque-Monsieur. Il est... délicieux/horrible. Il est facile/difficile à faire.

Work at home

- Set a history research task for the children to discover the factual origins of Bastille Day.

- Explain that *le Croque-Madame* is a variation of the classic *le Croque-Monsieur* sandwich. Challenge the children to find out how it differs. (It has a fried egg on top.)

- Ask the children to make an illustrated menu showing the two sandwiches in the previous activity. Underneath they should write which they prefer. (*Je préfère ...*) Can they persuade their parents to let them help make it?

- Give the children photocopiable 13B, a list of useful imperative verbs and food vocabulary (perhaps their food dictionaries from **Work at school**) to take home. Ask them to create a recipe for a salad (fruit or vegetable), try it out, and write a rough draft before they complete photocopiable 13B.

The Bastille, a prison in Paris, was the scene of the beginning of the French Revolution in 1789.

Unit 14 – Je suis le musicien

('I am the music man')

Unit theme
● Responding to music

Teaching points
● Offering opinions (about music)

● Making simple statements (about musical instruments)

● Expressing future intentions (about playing a musical instrument)

Grammar
● *Jouer + du, de la* (with a musical instrument)

● Immediate future : *aller* + infinitive (*Je vais jouer, Je vais chanter*)

Language sounds
● phoneme *qu*

● word ending *–ique*

Vocabulary

Tu joues ...?	Do you play ...?
Je joue du (saxophone/ piano/violon)	I play the (saxophone/ piano/violin) (m)
Je joue de la (guitare/ clarinette/batterie)	I play the (guitar/ clarinet/ drums) (f)
Qu'est-ce que tu vas faire?	What are you going to do?
Je vais jouer du... / de la...	I am going to play the ...
Je vais chanter	I am going to sing
C'est génial!	It's brilliant!
C'est nul/affreux/ennuyeux!	It's rubbish/awful/boring!
comme	like
la musique jazz	jazz music
la musique reggae	reggae music
la musique pop	pop music
la musique classique	classical music
la musique folklorique	folk music
Je préfère	I prefer
un saxophone	a saxophone
un piano	a piano
un violon	a violin
une guitare	a guitar
une clarinette	a clarinet
la batterie	the drums

Additional vocabulary for teachers

C'est quel genre de musique?	What kind of music is it?
Qu'est-ce que tu vas faire?	What are you going to do?
Il y a...	There is... / There are...
Battez la mesure/Bats la mesure	Beat time (plural/singular)
Changez/Change de temps	Change (plural/singular) the beat
Combien de pulsations comptez-vous?	How many beats can you count?
Bonne chance	Good luck

Resources
Separate pieces of music: at least one example of classical, jazz, folk, reggae, pop
Musical instruments (or pictures)

Lesson 1 C'est la musique! (It's music!)
Resources
Separate pieces of music to listen to with at least one example of each style: classical, jazz, folk, reggae, pop.

● Tell the children to prepare for a musical extravaganza!

● Write these five style names on the whiteboard: *la musique jazz; la musique reggae; la musique pop; la musique classique la musique folklorique*. Read them aloud for the children to repeat. Can they guess the meanings?

● Give everyone a piece of paper divided into five squares. Play the pieces of music, pausing after each for partners to hold whispered discussions about which style they think has just been played.

- Re-play the music pieces in the same order, pausing after each for the children to write a style's name.

- Confirm answers and find out who are the music experts!

- Bring out Jacques, your class puppet, and ask him: *Tu aimes la musique pop?* (Do you like pop music?) Disguising your voice, answer for him: *Oui, j'aime la musique pop.* Use the same question format to ask him about *la musique classique*, answering *Non, je n'aime pas la musique classique.*

- Let the children question a partner about their music tastes, always beginning *Tu aimes … ?*

- Revise the connectives *et* and *mais* (Unit 13, lesson 2). Write Jacques' two answers on the whiteboard and suggest creating one sentence. Which connective would be better? (*mais*) Demonstrate with *J'aime la musique pop mais je n'aime pas la musique classique.*

Follow-up
Using the last sentence as a model, let the children write a two-part sentence about their music tastes, using *J'aime...* and *je n'aime pas* (or *je préfère)...* and connecting with *mais*. When they read their sentence to a partner, are there any surprises?

Lesson 2 Je joue du piano! (I play the piano!)

Resources
These musical instruments (or pictures): saxophone, piano, violin, guitar, clarinet, drums.

- Take the class to the music room and show them these instruments: saxophone, piano, violin, guitar, clarinet, drums. (Alternatively, use pictures.)

- Put French labels by the instruments and model saying them.

- Make the names familiar by playing these variations of **What's my name?**

- Collect instrument labels so the class can help you re-place them.

- Collect and shuffle labels for individual children to pick and place one.

- Let the class vote with their *oui* or *non* card if the label is placed correctly.

- Mix up the labels, when the children's eyes are shut. Challenge a group to sort and place them within a time limit. Which group beats the clock?
- Say an instrument name for the children to represent it with the appropriate playing action.
- Hold up a label for the children to read aloud and point to the correct instrument.

- Play **Charades**, everyone secretly choosing an instrument to play in the orchestra. Choose someone to mime playing. Choose someone to ask the guessing question, for example: *Tu joues.. de la clarinette?* If correct, the miming player replies *Oui, je joue de la clarinette.* If incorrect, someone else asks the guessing question. Keep the game going with new players chosen to mime. Emphasise *jouer du* for masculine instruments and *jouer de la* for feminine.

- Play the separate music extracts from Lesson 1. Provide the construction *Il y a...* as the children write a sentence for each, identifying an instrument they can hear. For example: *1. Il y a une guitare.*

Follow-up
Use a simple tune for *Je joue du piano!* on photocopiable 14A. Divide the class into four groups and share out verses 2-5 to practise. Hold a class performance, everyone singing verses 1 and 6, separate groups singing and making appropriate playing actions and sounds for their verse.

Lesson 3
Battez la mesure (Beat time)

Resources
Photocopiable 14A; individual copies of the interview form in **Follow-up**

- Give the instruction *Battez la mesure* for the children to clap a beat.

- Hold another performance of *Je joue du piano!* (Photocopiable 14), the children joining you in clapping the beat. Between verses, alter the tempo with the instruction *Changez de temps.* Encourage the group that is singing to match the beat.

- Revise vocabulary as you ask children questions such as these:
  - *Comment tu t'appelles?*
  - *Tu aimes la musique jazz?*
  - *Tu joues du saxophone?*
  - *Tu aimes la musique classique?*
  - *Tu préfères la musique pop?*

- Explain that you will be holding a music contest, and are interviewing music groups to enter. Share and list on the whiteboard suggestions for group names, for example: *Les musiciens fantastiques!* The fantastic musicians!) *Les joueurs differents!* (The different players!) *Les lions* (The lions)

● Put the children into music groups of five to decide on their name and who will play which instrument. Suggest making notes, in French when possible, of their decisions.

● Warn them that you, as interviewer, will expect them all to speak! You may ask their name, their musical taste, what instrument they will play in the group, and the group's name. On the whiteboard, write sample questions and answer openers (See **Follow-up** and the vocabulary list on the Unit's opening page) so the children can prepare by doing partner conversations.

● Use Jacques, your class puppet, to demonstrate asking and answering a question about their future playing: *Qu'est-ce que tu vas faire?* (*Je vais jouer du saxophone.*)

● During conversation practice, move among groups, prompting ideas, adding vocabulary and guiding sentences.

● Hold the interviews (the class listening to each in turn). Announce your decision: every group has passed! They will all be in the music contest!

Follow-up
Create and print individual copies of this interview form. Let the children take turns interviewing a partner before they write their own answers:

o *Bonjour*

_____

o *Comment tu t'appelles ?*

_____

o *Et le groupe ?*

_____

o *Tu aimes la musique jazz?*

_____

o *Tu préfères la musique pop ?*

_____

o *Qu'est-ce que tu vas faire?*

_____

o *Bonne chance et au revoir!*

_____

Lesson 4 Le rap! (Rap)
Resources
Photocopiable 14B

● Remind the children about the forthcoming music contest and form the groups from Lesson 3. Use questions, for example those from Lesson 3's **Follow-up**, to revise group names and musician roles.

● Give the children photocopiable 14B and read and translate the words. Do a performance of the rap together.

● Suggest the rap needs one or two additional verses before finishing with a repetition of the first verse. The contest task is to compose and perform the extra verses!

● As groups compose, move among them, helping with vocabulary; suggest the use of word banks and dictionaries; and point out where poetic licence allows them to omit a word (as with *la mesure* in Verse 2, photocopiable 14B) to maintain the rhythm. Make sure that each group's organisation gives everyone involvement. (A group may work as a whole, or allocate some lines to some members.) Wordprocessing will make drafting and editing words easier.

● When verses are written, find a good space, perhaps the hall, for group rehearsals.

● Stage the contest! Make a recording as each group performs in turn, the rest of you listening and applauding. Encourage a positive attitude, as members of the audience make a secret note of their reaction to the rap and a score.

● At the end of the contest, hold a secret ballot and announce the winning group.

Follow-up
Display the words of the winning rap for a class performance. Find an occasion, perhaps a class assembly, for a performance for the school. Make a recording of the rap to exchange with a partner school's music. Consider putting material on the school's website.

France is a country of music lovers. French people enjoy listening to different types of music from all around the world. Summer music festivals are very popular.

Un, deux, trois!

Je joue du piano!

1. Je suis un musicien
Et je joue du piano!
Pia-pia-piano, piano, piano
Pia-pia-piano, piano, piano
Je joue du piano!

2. Je suis un musicien
Et je joue du violon!
Vio-vio-violon, violon, violon
Vio-vio-violon, violon, violon
Je joue du violon!

3. Je suis un musicien
Et je joue de la clarinette!
Clari-clari-clarinette, clarinette, clarinette
Clari-clari-clarinette, clarinette, clarinette
Je joue de la clarinette!

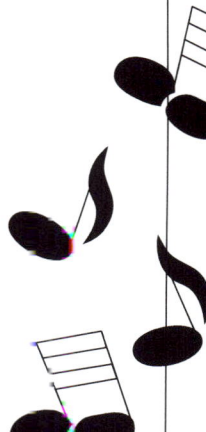

4. Je suis un musicien
Et je joue de la batterie!
Batter-batter-batterie, batterie, batterie
Batter-batter-batterie, batterie, batterie
Je joue de la batterie!

5. Je suis un musicien
Et je joue du saxophone!
Saxo-saxo-saxophone
Saxo-saxo-saxophone
Je joue du saxophone!

6. Je suis un musicien
Et je joue du piano!
Pia-pia-piano, piano, piano
Pia-pia-piano, piano, piano
Je joue du piano!

Le rap

Donc aujourd'hui,
Nous faisons un rap!
C'est très facile,
Nous faisons un rap!

D'abord, d'abord,
Battez mesure.
Combien de temps
Comptez-vous ?

Un, deux, trois, quatre
C'est la mesure.
Ne changez pas.
C'est la mesure.

Ecrivez ! Ecrivez !
Choisissez les mots!
Sur quel sujet?
N'importe lequel!

Mots sur la musique,
Mots sur le groupe.
Les mots génials !
Bonne chance ! Bonne chance !

Translation

So today, we're doing a rap.
It's very easy, we're doing a rap!

First of all, first of all, beat time.
How many beats do you count?

One, two, three, four, that's the beat.
Don't change it. That's the beat.

Write! Write! Choose the words.
On what subject? It doesn't matter what!

Words about music, words about the group,
Brilliant words! Good luck! Good luck!

More ideas for ...

Work at school

- Make links between French lessons and music lessons by choosing further examples of music for the children to listen to. Encourage careful listening and attention to detail as they decide which French music style label applies.

- Play the children a short piece of music every day. Let them listen to a short partner conversation between you and your Teaching Assistant about it. (You could prepare and record this in advance.) Then ask the children to hold similar partner or small group conversations about the music. Extend vocabulary by sometimes including a new target phrase or word of the day: for example, *Je préfère; Je déteste; C'est génial!; C'est nul/affreux/ennuyeux!;*

- Play **Going shopping!** Give partners the roles of a music shop retailer and a customer who comes in hoping to buy a CD.

  Provide these words as the framework starter, giving the children their conversation part on a small cue card. Can the partners continue the conversation? Will the customer leave with or without a CD?

  Customer: Bonjour
  Shop assistant: Bonjour.
  Customer: Je voudrais un CD.
  Shop assistant: Vous aimez la musique folklorique?
  Customer: Oui, mais je préfère la musique...

Work at home

- Give the children photocopiable 14B to take home and perform for a family audience. Suggest they ask family members to help them compose an additional verse or a new short rap about the family. At school, make a grand display of the work under the title *C'est le rap!*

- Ask the children to research current pop stars in France. Are French singers popular in this country as well? Do they always sing in French? Have the children heard of any English pop stars who have recorded songs in French? Suggest the children ask their family what they have heard. The children could present their findings in the format of a pop music magazine.

- Give the children a copy of this shop conversation in a play. Explain that the characters are saying their own words, but not in the correct places! Can the children write the conversation in the correct order?

  Customer: Bonjour
  Shop assistant: Au revoir
  Customer: Non, je déteste le jazz!
  Customer: Je voudrais un CD.
  Shop assistant: Vous aimez la musique jazz?
  Customer: Merci.
  Shop assistant: Vous aimez la musique folklorique?
  Customer: Au revoir
  Shop assistant: Bonjour
  Shop assistant: Voici un bon CD de la musique pop.
  Customer: Oui, mais je préfère la musique pop.

- Remind the children about their music group from lessons 3 and 4. Their group certainly needs publicity. Suggest making an advertising poster with pictures of them, their instruments, and the group's name.

George Bizet is a famous French composer. His opera, Carmen, is one of the most popular operas in the world today. Bizet lived in the 19th century and was a child prodigy: he started studying at the Conservatoire de Paris when he was only nine! (The Paris Conservatoire is a music college teaching music of the highest standards.)

Unit 15 – En route pour l'école

(On the way to school)

Unit theme
- Getting to school

Teaching points
- Describing a journey to school

- Local places

- Simple directions

- Telling the time on the half-hour

- The alphabet

Grammar
- Using *il y a*

- Using adverbial time phrases

Language sounds
Matching letter strings to sounds

Vocabulary

Quand je vais à l'école...	When I go to school...
Je passe devant...	I pass in front of...
cinq minutes plus tard	five minutes later
finalement	finally

vrai	true
faux	false
Il est une heure et demie, deux heures et demie, etc	It is half past one, half past two, etc
Je vais à l'ecole à huit heures et demie, etc	I go to school at half past eight, etc
à droite	(to/on the) right
à gauche	(to/on the) left
tout droit	straight ahead
Je ne comprends pas	I don't understand
Répétez s'il vous plaît	Repeat, please
un magasin	a shop
un café	a café
un musée	a museum
une poste	a post office
une rivière	a river
une gare	a train station
une église	a church

Additional language for teachers

Numéro... c'est quelle lettre?	Number... which letter is it?
la case	the square (in a grid)
A quelle heure vas-tu à l'école?	What time do you go to school?
Je traverse	I cross
après ça	after that
le passage pour piétons	the pedestrian crossing

Lesson 1 C'est quelle lettre? (Which letter is it?)

Resources
One copy of photocopiable 15A; a beanbag or soft ball
- Write the alphabet on the whiteboard and, using photocopiable 15A, Part 1 as your pronunciation guide, say the letters in French, the children repeating them after you.

- Arrange the whiteboard letters into the **Alphabet rap!** shown on the photocopiable. Sing the rap with the children, emphasising rhymes.

- Divide the class into groups, assigning each a section of the **Alphabet rap!** When possible, match the number of letters and group members, but some children may have to share a letter.

- Let group members work out who will sing or chant what. Will they have individual singers or chant letters together?

- Hold a class performance of the **Alphabet rap!** With every group singing on cue.

- Check attendance figures by playing **Number Ping-pong**. With everyone standing, point to someone to start counting: they say *un* and point to someone to carry on. After saying a number and 'batting' it to a successor, children can sit down. Play again, starting with someone else to make sure your attendance record is accurate.

Un, deux, trois!

- Progress to counting in tens from 10 to 100. (See Units 2, 8 and 9) with a game of **Beanbag challenge**. Form a class circle, you in the centre with a bean bag. Toss the bag to someone, at the same time calling out a multiple of 10: they throw it back to you, saying the next multiple of 10 or they are out.

- Return to the letters on the whiteboard and assign each, in alphabetical order, a number between 1 and 26.

- Combine numbers and letters oral work by asking, for example, *Numero 15, c'est quelle lettre?* In response, the children write on their individual whiteboards and say the letter o.

Follow-up

Put the children into pairs to play **Combination code.** Using photocopiable 15A, Part 2, read aloud sets of number words, the children writing them as numerals. Ask them to hold up their answers before you reveal the correct numerals. Leave these combinations on display for **Codebreakers**, the children using the alphabet-number code to decipher the secret words. Challenge the children to make encrypted secret words or a short message to try on a partner. Will anyone vary the alphabet-number code? (For example, change the direction of the numbering).

Lesson 2 Vrai ou faux? (True or false?)

Resources

Symbols to represent places; a pointing arrow; paper with large squares

- Display an empty grid of 6 x6 large squares. (You could create this on an interactive whiteboard.)

- Label the horizontal axis of the grid with the letters **A - F**; label the vertical axis with the numbers **1-6**.

- Put your pointer on a square and ask for its coordinates, its horizontal axis first. Demonstrate saying and writing an answer, for example *la case B, 2.* Get everyone talking by encouraging partners to tell each other their answer before you accept answers.

- Progress to naming coordinates, the children working out which square you are referring to and where the pointer should go.

- Explain that this grid is to help you plan and locate places in a town centre.

- Display map symbols for your places, naming the places for the children to repeat: *un magasin, un café, un musée, une poste, une église, une gare, une rivière.* Make the vocabulary familiar by playing **Read my lips** in which you mouth the word and the children say it aloud.

- Place symbols on your grid and make statements: for example, *Il y a un café dans la case C 3.* Each time, the children must decide if your statement is true or false, answering with *vrai* or *faux.*

- Progress to longer answers: *Oui, il y a un café* or *Non, il y a une rivière.* (If the grid is an interactive whiteboard, conceal places with a special screen. When children answer, erase the screen and reveal what is there.)

- Make regular changes to places and grid locations, and let children take your role.

Follow-up

Ask the children to make a similar grid and place symbols for their town layout. Underneath their grid they should write some mixed true and false *Il y a...* statements and their coordinates. Will a partner spot which to say *vrai* to, which *faux*?

Lesson 3 En route pour l'école (On the way to school)

Resources

Six large cards and six small cards with place names from Lesson 2; a prepared route for a journey to school passing known places; prepared journey descriptions

- Revise the place names from Lesson 2 with these games:
  - **Read my lips**: mouth the word for the children to say aloud.
  - **Show me**: Put the children into groups, each child drawing one place symbol. Say a place name. Does the correct group member stand up?
  - **Stop the bus!**
    1. Hang large place card names place names at different locations in the room.
    2. Explain they are also bus stops in the town.
    3. Play music, the children bustling around town.
    4. Pause the music for everyone to choose a bus stop to wait at.
    5. Holding your small place name cards instruct someone: *Prends une carte* (Take a card) and read it out.
    6. Passengers waiting there are out: this bus does not stop there!

- Keep re-starting the game, the remaining children choosing a bus stop each time the music pauses and a new card picked. After five journeys, who kept choosing a good stop?

- On the whiteboard, draw a simple map of a journey, place symbols marked. Add a house (*une maison*) to the beginning of the map, a school (*une école*) to the end. (Save this map to re-use in Lesson 4).

- Explain that the map shows your journey to school. Indicate relevant parts as you say: *Quand je vais a l'école, je passe devant une gare. Je passe devant un café.*

- Introduce time into the description: *Quand je vais a l'école, je passe devant une gare. <u>Cinq minutes plus tard</u> je passe devant un café. <u>Finalement</u> j'arrive à l'école.*

- Re-read your last description for groups to mime actions and locations.

Follow-up

Give the children an enlarged copy of Photocopiable 15B, Part 1 to do. Make a preliminary oral reading of Jacques' words with the children and display a dictionary bank of new vocabulary.

Lesson 4
Quelle heure est-il?
(What time is it?)

Resources

The class puppet; Map and journey description from Lesson 3; a large teaching clock with movable hands; small teaching clocks for the children (if available)

- Use a teaching clock to revise (from Unit 11) time on the hour. Practise the question *Quelle heure est-il?* and the answer *Il est ..... dix heures.*

- Bring out Jacques, your puppet. Encourage the class to ask him *Quelle heure est-il?*

- As Jacques alters the hands to half-past 10, let him answer (through you) *Il est dix heures et demie.*

- Repeat Jacques' game with other half-past times. Progress to a child re-setting the time (only to a time on the half hour) and the class saying it.
- Write four time statements. Can the children show or draw the clocks? Reverse the activity: draw a clock and let the children write the time statements.

- Play your special version of **What's the time Mr Wolf?** from Unit 11, Lesson 3. With you as lion, the children must listen for half hours as well as hours. (A half hour will need half a pace.) Emphasise that your animal noise (*roarr!*) means they must vanish!

- Ask Jacques *A quelle heure vas-tu à l'école?* Answer for him: for example, *Je vais à l'école à sept heures et demie.* Let partners exchange this information saying, to the nearest half hour, when they set off for school.

- Show the children your journey map from Lesson 3. Add a clock and a sentence to your house symbol. For example: *Je vais à l'école à ... sept heures.* Similarly, add a clock and sentence to your school symbol. For example: *J'arrive à l'école à ... sept heures et demie.* Can the children suggest other points on your map for a clock face and time statement?

- Use Photocopiable 15B, Part 2 for the children to make a simple map of their journey to school, marking places with symbols and important time(s) with clock faces. (Emphasise keeping to the nearest half hour).

Follow-up

Ask the children to write a short piece of text to explain their journey. Put useful vocabulary on display. Let the children make a presentation of their audio visual material to the class; less confident children may prefer to present their work to a partner or small group.

In France the school day starts at 8.30am and finishes at 4.30pm. At secondary school the day is longer: it starts at 8.00am and finishes at 5.00pm.

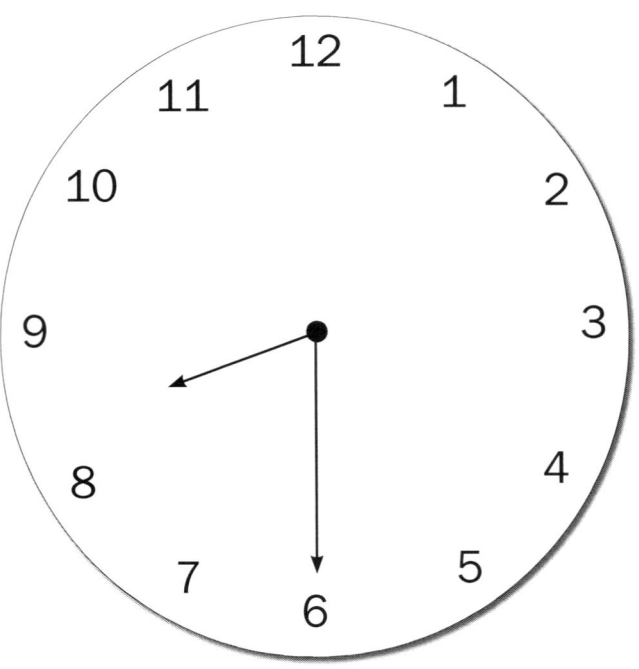

Un, deux, trois!

Alphabet rap!

a (ah) **b** (bay)	**c** (say) **d** (day)	**e** (eh) **f** (eff) **g** (zhay)	**h** (osh) **i** (ee)	**j** (zhee)
k (kah)	**l** (el) **m** (em)	**n** (en) **o** (oh) **p** (pay)	**q** (kew)	**r** (air) **s** (ess) **t** (tay)
u (ew)	**v** (vay)	**w** (doo-bleh vay)	**x** (eeks) **y** (ee-grek)	**z** (zed)

Combination codes

Number groups:

Deux, dix-huit, un, vingt-deux, quinze

Vingt-deux, quinze, neuf, trois, neuf

Treize, cinq, dix-huit, trois, dix-neuf

Douze, vingt-et-un, quatorze, quatre, neuf

Quatorze, quinze, dix-huit, quatre

Codebreakers

Combination codes

2, 18, 1, 22, 15

22, 15, 9, 3, 9

13, 5, 18, 3, 9

12, 21, 14, 4, 9

14, 15, 18, 4

Secret words: *bravo, voici, merci, lundi, nord*

Je vais à l'école

Read Jacques' description of his journey from home to school.
Write in his missing time phrases.
Draw a map to help others follow his route.

> *Quand je vais à l'école,*
> *je passe devant deux magasins.*
> _____
> *je passe devant une église.*
> *Après ça je passe devant une poste*
> *et puis une gare. _____,*
> *j'arrive à l'école.*

Finalement

Cinq minutes plus tard

Draw a map of your journey from home to school.
Write a description of the journey.
Include at least one time and one time phrase.

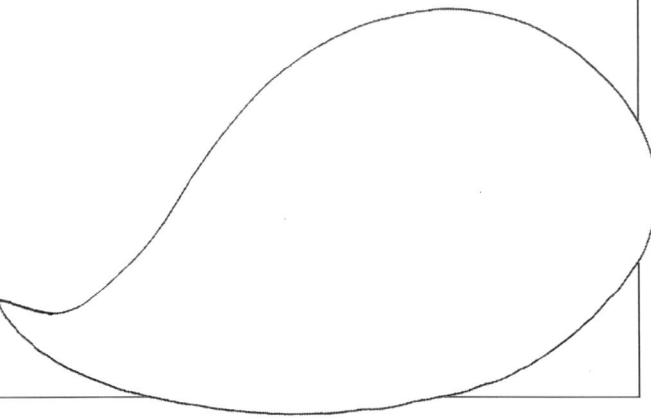

More ideas for...

Work at school

- Make **Alphabet rap!** a class favourite by holding regular performances. Incorporate audio and visual elements so the children say and see letters. Learning and remembering the alphabet will become easy and fun. Practise the alphabet with children spelling out a famous person's initials or full name. Can others work out the identity?

- Extend your work on school journeys to include mode of travel. Revise the relevant vocabulary from Unit 7 and the question *Comment vas-tu à l'école?* and answers such as *Je vais à l'école à pied.* Suggest the children add this information to their writing from Lesson 4's **Follow-up**.

- Teach the children these directions: *à droite; à gauche; tout droit*. Provide plenty of space in a game of **Follow your nose**: you call out a series of directions, using imperatives; the children have to finish up facing the correct way. Directions could include: *Tournez... à gauche. Allez... tout droit.* Make the game more fun by creating 'places' in the room: for example, *un café*. Play the game again. Will your directions take them to the right place? Challenge the children to direct a partner to a place. Add new vocabulary: *le passage pour piétons* and *traversez*.

- Improve the children's speaking, listening and spelling by displaying a short account of your journey. Omit letter strings from some words. Read the account aloud, asking children to write and hold up the missing letter strings on their individual whiteboards when you reach those words.

Work at home

- Create a worksheet of shopping bags, each containing a muddled version of one of these sentences:
  Je vais à l'école à huit heures.
  Je vais a l'école à pied.
  Il y a un café en route pour l'école.
  Je passe devant un bureau de poste.
  Il y a un passage pour piétons.
  Je traverse la rue au passage pour piétons.
  Finalement j'arrive à l'école.
  J'arrive à l'école à huit heures et demie.

- Give each child a copy of the worksheet. Ask them to cut out each shopping bag, take out and sort the bag's words and write them as a sentence. Challenge them to prove their understanding by adding illustrations.

- Ask the children to draw a simple map of a journey they make from home to a local shop. Give them a vocabulary list so they can write a description of their journey - the places they pass and the directions they follow. Include sentence-starters and helpful phrases in the vocabulary list. For example: *Quand je vais au magasin...; je passe devant...; je tourne...; je traverse...*

- Give the children a page of clock faces and a list of time sentences. Can the children match each clock to its time sentence?

L'école primaire (Primary school) is for children from six to eleven. School years are counted in the opposite way to Britain's: six-year-olds are in Year 11; eleven-year-olds are in Year 7.

Unit 16 – Scène de plage

(Beach scene)

Unit theme
- Looking at a painting (of a beach)

Teaching points
- Describing a scene or place

- Using adjectives to add interest and detail

- Writing instructions

Grammar
- Regular -er verbs (third person singular, present tense)

- *Dormir* (third person singular, present tense: *il/elle dort*)

- Imperatives: *tu* form

- *C'est, Ce n'est pas* + noun

Language sounds
- *au/eau*

- *il, ille*

Vocabulary

(Le chien) regarde	(The dog) is watching
(Le bateau) glisse	(The boat) is gliding along
(La petite fille) dort	(The little girl) is sleeping
(La dame) brosse (les	(The lady) is brushing
cheveux de la petite fille)	(the little girl's hair)
Les gens marchent/ parlent/jouent	The people are walking/ talking/playing
C'est ...	It is ...
Ce n'est pas ...	It is not ...

(Instructions are given in the familiar/singular form)

prends	take
ajoute	add
mélange	mix
décore	decorate
laisse	leave
le sable	the sand
le ciel	the sky
le bateau	the boat
la mer	the sea
la plage	the beach
une baie	a bay
une falaise	a cliff
une grotte	a cave
des coquillages	(m) shells
des rochers	(m) rocks
des cailloux	(m) pebbles

Additional vocabulary for teachers

On va jouer au Morpion	We're going to play **Noughts and Crosses**
Que fait le bateau / la petite fille / la dame?	What is the boat /little girl / lady doing?
Que font les gens?	What are the people doing?

Resources
A photocopy of a painting of a beach scene (for example, *Scène de plage* by Degas)

Lesson 1 Scène de plage (Beach scene)

Resources
A coloured copy of a beach scene (preferably *Scène de plage* by Degas); large PE hoops in assorted colours; coloured PE bands

- Put a mixture of red, blue, yellow and green large PE hoops on the floor.

- Revising colour vocabulary from Unit 4, call out a colour, for example *rouge*. Watch to see who moves next to or into a red hoop.

- Change the hoops to piles of PE bands. Call out a colour, for example *jaune*: if children go and put on a yellow band, they are in the correct team!

- On the whiteboard, create a colour chart: black, white, brown, violet, orange and pink.

- Put the children into pairs. Choosing a pair, give the instruction, for example, *Touchez rose*. If they touch pink, they win a point.

- Display a coloured copy of a beach scene painting (preferably *Scene de plage* by Degas**)**

- Identify about eight relevant, important nouns in the painting: for example *le sable, le chien, le bateau* and *la mer*. Write the words and let the children practise saying them.

- Play class **Pictogram**, in which you say a descriptive colour sentence about an item in the painting: for example, *La mer est verte* (The sea is green) Challenge the children to quickly draw and colour what you describe.

- Put the children into pairs or small groups for small games of **Pictogram**, individuals or pairs writing a secret, descriptive colour sentence about the painting, and taking turns reading it to the rest of the group. Will the others draw and colour what the writer meant?

Follow-up
Suggest the children make a list (in English) of 10 nouns represented in the painting that they do not know the French words for. Give them bilingual dictionaries so they can write the French equivalents.

Lesson 2 Que fait le chien? (What is the dog doing?)

Resources
Two cardboard dice: one dice with a colour word written on each face, the other with a noun from Lesson 1 on each face

- Revise the noun and colour vocabulary from Lesson 1 with this game:
  - Have two large dice: one dice with a colour word written on each face; the other dice with one of the nouns from Lesson 1 on each face.
  - Put the children into pairs. Roll both dice and choose two children to work together to put the words showing into a sentence. Does the class know what the children say?

- Display the Degas painting again and introduce some verbs relevant to its action. For example, say *La petite fille dort.* Then ask the question *Que fait la petite fille?* so the children repeat the answer *La petite fille dort.* Do this with other questions and answers: (*Que fait le bateau ?*) *Le bateau glisse;* (*Que fait le chien?*) *Le chien regarde;* (*Que fait la dame?*) *La dame brosse les cheveux de la petite fille.*

- Use the plural question form for *les gens* in the picture asking *Que font les gens?* Introduce answers such *Les gens marchent.*

- Make the children familiar with the verbs' meanings by playing these games:
  - Call out one of the sentences for the class to mime.
  - Let individuals replace you as caller and say one of the sentences for the class to mime.
  - Divide the class into five groups. Give each group a role in the picture: *le chien, la petite fille, la dame, le bateau, les gens*. Ask the groups to freeze-frame their part. Write their five answer sentences on the whiteboard. In turn, bring groups to life to say their sentence.

- Read aloud this new word scene so everyone can act what is happening now.
  La dame dort.
  Le chien marche.
  Les gens parlent.
  La petite fille brosse les cheveux de la dame.
  Le bateau glisse.

Follow-up
Write the above description on the whiteboard. Write a box of nouns and verbs at the side. Ask the children to create and write their own new beach scene and draw the beach scene to fit their writing.

Lesson 3 La plage (The beach)

Resources
The copy of the painting being studied; individual copies of Photocopiable 16A; UK tourist board websites with images of popular UK beaches

- Display the Degas painting and some sentences from the end of Lesson 2:

  Le chien marche. La petite fille brosse les cheveux de la dame. Le bateau glisse.

- Ask partners to work on one sentence at a time, adding a colour description to each sentence. Choose an answer and amend your written sentence accordingly: for example. *Le chien vert marche. La petite fille brosse les cheveux noirs de la dame. Le bateau rouge glisse.*

- Highlight the colour descriptions. Ask: What type of words are they? (Adjectives) Can you identify an adjective already in one sentence? (petite)

- Point out the position of the colour adjectives: they follow the nouns they describe. Explain that this is the adjective's usual position in French, but there are many exceptions (such as *grand, petit*, and numbers) that precede the noun.
- Ask: What happens to an adjective's spelling? Emphasise its agreement with its noun: *noirs* and *petite*.

- Give the children further oral practice by creating sentences about the painting, the children adding adjectives. Demonstrate the adjectives' spelling.

- Examine the physical details of the painting's beach and setting. Ask: Are there resemblances to seaside places you know in the UK and French-speaking countries?

- Use Internet tourist board sites to show images of well-known English beaches: for example, Bournemouth, Brighton and Torquay. Consider typical physical characteristics, finding opportunities to introduce these words: *une falaise* (a cliff); *une baie* (a bay); *une grotte* (a cave); *des coquillages* (shells); *des rochers* (rocks); *des cailloux* (pebbles). List and say the words for the children to repeat after you.

- Display an enlarged picture of one popular English beach. Ask the children questions to elicit affirmative answers: for example, *C'est une baie? Oui, c'est une baie. Il y a des coquillages? Oui, il y a des coquillages.* Elicit a negative response: for example, *Il y a du sable? Non, il y a des cailloux.*

- Finish by displaying and reading aloud the poem on the top section of Photocopiable 16A. Create a glossary next to the poem with the meanings of some unfamiliar words. Explain the construction *aussi... que* (as... as).

Follow-up
Give the children a copy of Photocopiable 16A to follow the words as you read the poem aloud again, encouraging them to join in. Leave the glossary on display as partners do the work on the photocopiable.

Lesson 4 Mélange une plage! (Mix a beach!)

Resources
One copy of Photocopiable 16A; individual copies of Photocopiable 16B
- Display and read aloud the poem *La plage* from Photocopiable 16A.

- Let the children use their answers to the questions on the bottom half of the photocopiable as you discuss the poem and its meaning:

The Beach
The blue sky is as calm as the sea. The calm sea is as large as the sand. The large sand is as golden as the sun. The golden sun is as gleaming as the shells. The gleaming shells are as white as the clouds. The white clouds are as silent as the boats. The silent boats are as blue as the sky. It is perfect on the beach.

- Highlight changes in adjectives' spelling (for example, *grande* to *grand*; *bleus* to *bleu*) to accommodate noun changes: feminine to masculine, plural to singular.

- Point out similes in the poem and the French construction *aussi... que...* (as... as...).

- Write, say and explain these imperative verbs: *prends; ajoute; mélange; décore; laisse.*

- Agree on actions as you test the children's memories in these games:
  o **Cook together** Call out an imperative for everyone to obey. Have quick changes of action. Do some chefs go wrong?
  o **Do your bit** Put the children into five groups, numbering each group. Call out a group's number and imperative. When every group is performing, check to see who is messing up the recipe by not following their instruction.
  o **Watch my lips** Keep the children in five groups. Visit each group in turn, silently mouthing an imperative. Does every group do the correct action?

- Suggest using these imperatives to start lines in a class poem about a beach. (You could use the Degas painting, a postcard scene, an imaginary beach.)

- Work together to construct and write simple lines. Give time for partner or small group discussion before you ask for and accept ideas. Encourage the addition of adjectives and detail. Talk about an ending. Will you name your beach? For example:

Prends du sable jaune et un soleil brillant.
Ajoute une mer calme et un petit bateau vert.
Mélange avec un garçon qui nage.
Décore avec des beaux coquillages.
Laisse au soleil pendant une semaine.
Voila la plage à Bournemouth !

- Read the poem together. Do the children have a mental picture of the beach?

Follow-up
Give the children Photocopiable 16B to use the same recipe format to write their own beach poem. Suggest working in pairs, doing initial drafts and using the class poem for guidance.

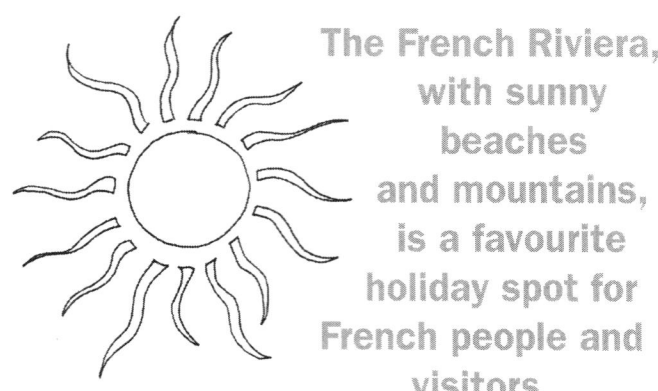

The French Riviera, with sunny beaches and mountains, is a favourite holiday spot for French people and visitors.

Un, deux, trois!

La plage

Le ciel bleu est aussi calme que la mer.
La mer calme est aussi grande que le sable.
Le grand sable est aussi doré que le soleil.
Le soleil doré est aussi brillant que les coquillages.
Les coquillages brillants que sont aussi blancs que les nuages.
Les nuages blancs sont aussi silencieux que les bateaux.
Les bateaux silencieux sont aussi bleus que le ciel.
C'est parfait sur la plage.

Read the poem with your partner. Discuss each question before you write an answer.

What is the poem about?

Find three reasons why the poet likes the beach.

Which French colour adjective describes the boat?

What two items are described as blancs?

List six other adjectives in the poem.

What is the sand compared to?

Why does the poet make this comparison?

Mélange une plage...

Ajoute… _____

_____

Mélange… _____

_____

Décore… _____

_____

Laisse… _____

_____

More ideas for...

Work at school

- In a dance lesson, put the children into small groups to plan and perform a sequence of movements that bring the Degas painting to life.

- Give the children the top half of photocopiable 16A. Ask them to underline or circle, in different colours, the words containing:
  1. the grapheme *au* and *eau*;
  2. the grapheme *il* and *ille*;

- Let the children listen as you say the words. Can they hear the differences in pairs of sounds? Working on one pair of sounds at a time, agree on an action (such as thumb up or thumb down) for children to use when they hear that sound in an assortment of words you read aloud. Award 'Great listener!' badges.

- Hold a poetry festival in which everyone takes the role of both performer and audience: partners read aloud their poems from the **Follow-up** to Lesson 4 to a group or the whole class. Encourage the audience to listen carefully for the colours being painted by the poems.

- Suggest that the children do a painting or postcard to illustrate their 'beach recipe' poem, written in the **Follow-up** to Lesson 4. Create a display of the pictures and words.

Work at home

- Ask the children to see what they can find out, using books or the Internet, about Degas and his painting *Scène de plage*. Is there a painting with the same title by another artist? Suggest they use an art book to find three other beach paintings they find appealing, and list their titles and artists.

- Ask the children to bring from home a favourite photograph they, or a family member, has taken of a beach they like in the UK or a French-speaking country. Invite the children to show and talk about this beach to a partner or group, explaining what they like.

- Provide the children with a vocabulary sheet so that they can compose a short paragraph in French about one of their favourite beaches (perhaps the beach in the photograph in the previous activity.) Provide helpful sentences starters they may choose to use:
  - **C'est la plage à...** (for example, **Blackpool**)
  - **Le sable est...**
  - **Il y a...**
  - **J'aime beaucoup...**

Paris is an inland city, but each summer an artificial beach is created in the city so that people can enjoy the feeling of being on the beach.

Unit 17 – Les quatre saisons

(The four seasons)

Unit theme
- Responding to a poem

Teaching points
- Describing the weather (present and past)

- Using adjectives as antonyms

Grammar
- Prepositions: *en, au* (with the seasons)

- Adjectives: position and agreement

- Imperfect verb tense (For example, *il faisait chaud*)

Language sounds
- Matching sounds to writing

Vocabulary

l'hiver	winter
le printemps	spring
l' été (m)	summer
l' automne	autumn
au printemps	in spring
en été/automne/hiver	in summer/autumn/winter
il faisait beau	it was good weather
il faisait mauvais	it was bad weather
il faisait froid	it was cold
il faisait du vent	it was windy
il faisait du soleil	it was sunny
clair	light
sombre	dark
heureux	happy
triste	sad
J'ai visité	I visited
coloré	colourful
fade	dull
agité	excited
calme	calm
rigolo	funny
sérieux	serious
Viens/Reste chez moi	Come to /stay (singular) with me
Les couleurs sont …	The colours are
Tape les mains /	Clap (singular) your hands
les pieds	/tap (singular) your feet

Habitats could include:

la prairie	the meadow
l'étang (m)	the pond
le parterre de fleurs	the flower bed
le jardin	the garden
la ferme	the farm
un écureuil	a squirrel
un papillon	a butterfly
une hirondelle	a swallow
une grenouille	a frog
une mouette	a seagull
un coccinelle	a ladybird
une guêpe	a wasp

Additional vocabulary for teachers

l'été dernier/prochain	last/next summer
la semaine dernière/ prochaine	last/next week
l'année dernière/ prochaine	last/next year
hier	yesterday
aujourd'hui	today
demain	tomorrow
C'est quelle saison?	What season is it?
Tout est...	Everything is...
Associez/Associe une couleur à une saison	Match (plural/singular) a colour to a season
Décrivez/Décris une saison	Describe (plural/singular) a season
Essuyez le tableau	Wipe the board
C'est de quelle couleur?	What colour is it?

Resources
A recording of Vivaldi's 'The Four Seasons';
the class puppet

Lesson 1
C'est quelle saison?
(What season is it?)

Resources
Class puppet; calendar pictures representative of the
time of year

- Revise the months of the year (See Unit 3) by chanting them in these groups, to a simple tune: *janvier, février; mars avril mai; juin, juillet, août; septembre, octobre, novembre; décembre.* Encourage the children to join in as you repeat the song.

- Ask the children to write their birthday month on their individual whiteboard. Sing the song again, this time children standing, holding up their whiteboard and singing alone when their month is reached.

- Announce that you are dividing the classroom into seasons. Hang signs in four different areas of the room: *l'hiver; le printemps; l'été; l'automne.*

- Go to each sign in turn, hold up a representative picture (for example a snowy field) and announce, for example, *l'hiver*, the children repeating the season after you.

- Display outdoor scenes where the weather and stage of plant or animal life are obvious. Ask *C'est quelle saison?* the children replying *C'est... (l'hiver).*

- Make statements about months and the season they are in: for example, *Février est en hiver; septembre est au printemps.*

- Make sure that you use example sentences that use *en hiver, au printemps, en été, en automne.* Point out the use of *en* and *au* to express in a season. Let the children repeat the four phrases after you.

- Tell the children which season your birthday is in: *Mon anniversaire est en hiver.* Bring out Jacques, your class puppet, to tell the children (via your disguised voice) his birthday season.

- Invite the children to tell a talk partner their birthday season. (Their whiteboard month label will let them help each other.)

- Ask the children to sit in the appropriate area of the room, taking their whiteboards labels with them as identification. Suggest checks: 'Are others in my month here? Which other months are in this area?'

- Play a game in which you hold up assorted calendar pictures. The correct season has only one minute to make its claim: *C'est... l'été.* If correct, they win the picture. Which season successfully claims most?

Follow-up
Suggest having a living interactive calendar of the four seasons. Challenge the groups to plan and practise a tableau, that will come to life and and make its statement (*C'est... l'été*) when you point the remote control at them. Hold a class performance of the cycle of the year's seasons.

The climate in many areas of France
is excellent for producing good wine.
Two of the best-known winemaking
areas are Beaujolais (near Lyon) and
Côtes du Rhône (southerly).

Lesson 2 L'été dernier... (Last summer...)

- Revise these weather phrases from Units 7 and 12: *Il fait beau* (It is good weather) *Il fait chaud* (It is hot) *Il pleut* (It is raining) *Il neige* (It is snowing). Explain that they are all in the present tense. Do the children know how to tell? (The verbs would tell them.)

- Display a postcard - perhaps of the Eiffel Tower in Paris. Write on the whiteboard: *L'été dernier, j'ai visité Paris. Il faisait chaud.*

- Read the text aloud. Let the children, in pairs, try to work out the meaning. Can they tell if the text is about the present, past or future? What clues can they find?

- Share thoughts and highlight the time clue *dernier* and the past tense verbs: *j'ai visité* and *Il faisait chaud.* Agree on the text's meaning. (Last summer, I visited Paris. It was hot.)

- Explain that *faisait* is the imperfect tense of the verb *faire*; the imperfect tense is used to describe weather in the past.

- Teach the children other weather phrases that use *faire* in the imperfect tense: *Il faisait mauvais / froid/ du vent /du soleil.* Use weather symbols as the children practise the phrases.

- Play a game with this equipment:
  - two small soft balls: a red one labelled 'present'; a blue one labelled 'past';
  - a pack of weather symbol cards. (Make sure they are types of weather that use *faire* in their weather phrase.)

- Put the children into pairs; throw one of them a ball; invite their partner to pick a (face down) weather card. Can the partners make a suitable weather phrase with the appropriate tense of *faire*? Give every pair a turn. How many pairs win a point?

Follow-up
Give the children photocopiable 17A to create and write sentences about last summer's holiday in France. Suggest the children work in pairs.

Lesson 3 Le retour de l'été (The return of summer)

Resources
Photocopiable 17B; an interactive whiteboard, if available
- Give the instructions *Tape les mains* (Clap your hands) and *Tape les pieds* (Tap your feet) demonstrating what they mean. Play **Which is which?** as you give sudden instructions, the children deciding quickly which action is needed.

- Read aloud the chorus of the French poem on photocopiable 17B, the children doing their actions. Did they hear which season was mentioned? (Summer)

- Display the whole poem and read it aloud, the children joining in and acting the chorus. Give time for partner discussion as you ask: What is the poem about? What things change in each verse? (The animal and the place)

- Examine the first verse. Highlight and read aloud *matin, viens* and *chemin.* Can the children suggest why the poet has used those words? Is it just chance? Read them again as talk partners discuss your questions. Suggest that the words improve the poem's rhythm by rhyming (they all have the sound *in*) and all having two syllables.

- Remove the poem from display and write these lines, in their muddled order, on the whiteboard. (Have the text ready on your interactive whiteboard.)
  Viens, viens, viens,
  Tape les mains
  Une abeille m'a dit « Viens,
  Dans le champ, ce matin
  C'est l'été qui revient.
  L'été est sur le chemin. »

- Colour code the lines by putting a different circle of colour next to each.

- Give the children, individually or in pairs, six separated, interlocking bricks of the equivalent colours.

- As you read the lines of the poem aloud in the correct order (from your copy of photocopiable 17B) the children must identify the line and its colour. Their aim is to finish with their bricks in the correct colour order. Read the lines more than once.

- Order the lines on the whiteboard as the children display their results. Were some lines easy to place? Which spoken words were easiest to match to their written forms?

Follow-up
Give the children the top half of photocopiable 17B. Ask them to underline the animal and its habitat in each verse. Suggest they make a glossary, listing these six nouns and their written and pictorial meanings. Give partners access to a bilingual dictionary as they work on adding an animal and place to the poem as they write an additional verse. (Animals could include: *une coccinelle* (a ladybird), *une guêpe* (a wasp), *une hirondelle* (a swallow). Habitats could include: *la prairie* (the meadow), *le parterre de fleurs* (the flower bed), *la ferme* (the farm).

Lesson 4 La saison préférée (The favourite season)

Resources

A recording of Vivaldi's 'The Four Seasons'

- Remind the children about the poem on photocopiable 17B about summer's return.

- Suggest that each season is like a person, persuading people that their season is best.

- Write *l'hiver; le printemps; l'été; l'automne* on four separate pieces of paper. Agree on and write persuasive words, phrases and lines *l'hiver* could say. For example:
  - *Viens, viens, viens,*
  - *L'hiver est très blanc.*
  - *L'hiver est sur le chemin.*
  - *Reste chez moi.*
  - *L'hiver est si frais.*

- Encourage the children to think about weather and colours as you write similar lines, phrases and single words for the other seasons. Suggest adjectives and sentence structures, and show how to adapt ideas and lines from the photocopiable poem.

- Re-form the birthday season groups used in Lesson 1, explaining that each season will try to persuade other people that their season is the best.

- Ask the children to make pairs or groups of three with children in their season and to decide on which persuasive sentence or phrases to say. Encourage originality.

- Give the children time to practise pronunciation, intonation and persuasive facial and body language.

- Ask two seasons – *l'hiver* and *l'été* - to form lines facing each other, an alley way between the lines, talk partners standing next to each other.

- Let the children in the other two groups walk down the alley, listening and watching as the children in *l'hiver* and *l'été* whisper their lines to them.

- Ask the children in *le printemps* and *l'automne* to vote for which season was more persuasive.

- Change roles: *le printemps* and *l'automne* form lines facing each other, an alley between, and *l'hiver* and *l'été* walk between the lines, listening and watching.

- Hold a final contest between the two winners. The class will discover which season they most look forward to returning.

Follow-up

Repeat the Conscience Alleys, Vivaldi's 'The Four Seasons' playing quietly in the background. Does the same season win?

Give the children written sentences to complete about the season they like:

J'aime _____. C'est si_____.
Invite them to extend the text.

(For example: *J'aime l'été . C'est si coloré. Il y a beaucoup de fleurs.*)

In summer, the Tour de France is held. The race takes three weeks and is very popular with spectators.

L'été dernier...

Make up six pairs of sentences about your imaginary trip around France last year. Each pair of sentences must say where you visited and what the weather was like.

Use this example to help you:

L'été dernier, j'ai visité Paris. Il faisait très chaud.

L'été dernier	Avignon	Il faisait chaud
j'ai visité	Bordeaux	Il faisait froid
	Nice	Il faisait du vent
	Marseille	Il faisait mauvais
	Toulouse	Il faisait du soleil
	Boulogne	Il faisait beau

Le retour de l'été

Dans le jardin, ce matin
Un papillon m'a dit « Viens,
Viens, viens, viens,
L'été est sur le chemin. »

Refrain
Tape les mains
C'est l'été qui revient.
Tape les pieds
C'est l'été qui recommence.

Dans le champ, ce matin
Une abeille m'a dit « Viens,
Viens, viens, viens,
L'été est sur le chemin. »

(Refrain)

Près de la rivière, ce matin
Une grenouille m'a dit « Viens,
Viens, viens, viens,
L'été est sur le chemin. »

The return of summer

In the garden this morning
A butterfly said to me, "Come,
Come, come, come,
Summer is on its way."

Chorus
Clap your hands
Summer is coming again.
Tap your feet
Summer is starting again.

In the field this morning
A bee said to me, "Come,
Come, come, come,
Summer is on its way."

(Chorus)

Near the river this morning
A frog said to me, "Come,
Come, come, come,
Summer is on its way."

More ideas for...

Work at school

- Practise the use of *faire* in the present and past tenses by playing **Today and Yesterday**:
  - One child says a weather sentence beginning with *Aujourd'hui*. (For example: *Aujourd'hui il fait du soleil.*)
  - Their partner replies with an *Hier...* sentence. (For example: *Hier il faisait froid.*)

- Expand the children's vocabulary by giving them this written list of adjectives:
  chaud, clair, heureux, sombre, coloré, rigolo, agité, triste, fade, calme, froid, sérieux.
  Give the children a bilingual dictionary to find out and write a meaning for each. Ask them to pair the adjectives into antonyms. Can they write any more pairs of antonyms?

- Follow up the last activity in **Work at home**, sharing ideas and working together on a class poem about the return of a different season.

- Use your Conscience Alley activity from Lesson 4 for a class performance. Put two seasons on either side of the alley and have only a few children (and perhaps yourself) walking through. Include Vivaldi's music, and indicate to the children when they should speak. Encourage clear speech and theatrical movements. Finish by the walkers declaring the class's favourite season: for example: *C'est l'automne. C'est la saison préférée.*

Work at home

- Give the children their list of adjectives and meanings from the second **Work at home** activity. Ask them to use the adjectives in written sentences, being careful about position and agreement. Suggest they try to make up sentences relating to the theme '*Les quatre saisons*'.

- Invite the children to create an unusual family album, in which they put a picture of each member of their family, pretend that the person is speaking for themselves in a speech bubble and add a written sentence stating their birthday season.
  Supply:
  - the sentence beginning: *Mon anniversaire est...*
  - the prepositions and seasons: *en hiver/été; au printemps/automne.*

- Ask the children to create a pictorial season wheel for the year. In each season, they should write a typical weather and two colours they associate with the season. Supply a vocabulary sheet to help.

- Give the children the French poem on photocopiable 17B. Ask them to plan how and where to change the poem so it is about the return of a different season. What and how many changes will they make?

Summer in the South of France is very hot and dry. Forest fires can be a danger.

Un, deux, trois!

Unit 18 – Les planètes

(The planets)

Unit theme
- The planets

Teaching points
- Describing a planet

- Making a statement about a planet's position

- Classifying nouns, adjectives and verbs

Grammar
- Using qualifiers: *assez*

- Using prepositions: *près de, loin de*

- Making compound sentences with *parce que*

Language sounds
Phonemes: revising and hearing common phonemes to help writing

Vocabulary

la Terre	the Earth
la lune	the moon
un nom	a noun
un nom propre	a proper noun
un adjectif	an adjective
parce que	because

elle	it (feminine) she
près de... (près du soleil)	near... (near the sun)
loin de... (loin du soleil)	far from... (far from the sun)
assez	quite
Mercure (f)	Mercury
Vénus (f)	Venus
Mars (f)	Mars
Jupiter (f)	Jupiter
Saturne (f)	Saturn
Uranus (f)	Uranus
Neptune (f)	Neptune
Pluton (f)	Pluto
à droite	to the right
à gauche	to the left

Additional vocabulary for teachers

Associez/Associe un jour	Match (plural/singular) a day
à une planète	with a planet
Soulignez/Souligne	Underline (plural/singular)
Décrivez/Décris	Describe (plural/singular)
le diable à ressort	the jack-in-the-box
ici	here
Je pense à...	I'm thinking of...
C'est quelle planète?	Which planet is it?
Pourquoi?	Why?

Resources
Pictures of the planets

Lesson 1 C'est quelle planète? (Which planet is it?)

Resources
Separate pictures of the planets; separate flashcards of each planet's name; copies of photocopiable 18A (enough for one between two children)

- Show a picture of each of the planets in turn, naming them orally: *Mercure, Vénus, la Terre, Mars,*

Jupiter, Saturne, Uranus, Neptune, Pluton. (The internet is a good source of pictures: for example, www.nasa.gov).

- Emphasise pronunciation, the children tapping the number of syllables. Always say the planets in the same order.

- Play **Write what you hear**: you say the name of a planet; the children write the word. Keep the activity fun with partner collaboration. Display a word card answer. Who was correct? Did they hear and spell a phoneme they recognised?

- Give time for pronunciation practice, partners taking turns to be speaker or listener.

- Ask nine children to stand facing the class. Shuffle the word cards and deal a card each, for the nine children to hold their planet name in front of them.

- Put the rest of the class into pairs. Let a pair of children at a time make one position change to the line of nine human planets as the class tries to order them. How many pairs will have to make a change? Play again with new human planets. Does the class order them more quickly?

- Put the children into pairs with one copy of photocopiable 18A, the cards cut out, for these games:
  - **Line them up**
    The children spread out their cards, names showing. Can they put the names in order? When they turn the cards over, do the numbers match the positions?
  - **What's my name?**
    With the cards in a pile, numbers up, the partners take turns trying to identify the planet belonging to the top card. If correct, that partner wins the card; if wrong, the card is returned, number up, to the bottom of the pile. How many planets do they each win?

- Finish with another game of **Write what you hear**. Have the children got better at recognising oral phonemes and relating them to writing?

Follow-up
Return to the partner game, **What's my name?** Suggest adding to its difficulty: a player only wins the card if they know the name of the planet and can pronounce it to their partner's satisfaction.

Lesson 2
Décrivez les planètes (Describe the planets)
Resources
Pictures of the planets in colour; a soft ball

- Revise the planets' names from Lesson 1. Play **Pass it on**: start a foam ball on a journey around the classroom; whoever catches it says the next planet in the sequence.

- Display pictures of some of the planets, asking the children simple questions about colour or size. For example:
  - *Mars est une planète rouge. Oui ou non?*
  - *Pluton est une planète grande ou petite ?*
  - *De quelle couleur est Jupiter?*
    Involve everyone by encouraging talk partners to answer each other before you accept an answer from someone.

- Write a description on the whiteboard: *Pluton est une planète petite. Mercure est une planète rapide. Mars est une planète rouge.*

- Ask the children to tell their partner a common noun in the text. Can they identify a proper noun? What adjectives can they point out to their partner?

- Invite some children to underline, in different colours, appropriate words in the whiteboard's text. Let the class read the words aloud.

- Challenge the children to work out an English translation of the text. Does their partner agree?

- Under the French text on the whiteboard, write the English translation. Ask the children's help in underlining the equivalent English common nouns, proper nouns and adjectives as underlined in the French version.

- Invite partners to discuss both texts, particularly the underlined words. Are the words in the two languages similar? What about their sentence positions? Can partners work out and write a rule to help writers who compose a descriptive sentence in French?

- Put the children into groups of six to listen to one another's rules.

- Let the children write a final version of their rule (and a descriptive sentence demonstrating the rule) for a 'Top writing tips' section on your French notice board.

Follow-up
Ask the children to write a descriptive text of two or three sentences about some planets. Most children should be able to write independently, using a partner as their checker. Less confident children may work in pairs.

Lesson 3
A droite ou à gauche? (To the right or to the left?)
Resources
Separate flashcards of each planet's name; a flashcard saying *le soleil*; sets of flashcards to form sentences (sentences supplied)

- Draw two direction arrows and write underneath: *à droite* (right) and *à gauche* (left).

- Select nine children to stand in line facing the class. Give them, in muddled order, the nine planet wordcards from Lesson 1.

- Indicate one human planet at a time for the class to call out the direction to move: *à droite; à gauche;* or *ici* (here). How long does it take to get the planets in order?

- Give a tenth child the wordcard *le soleil*. Where does the class want to position *le soleil* ? (At the start of the line, next to *Mercure*.)

- Select five children to stand facing the class and give them, in muddled order, the wordcards for *Pluton est une planète petite*. Let the class call out directions to order the human sentence. Repeat this with the other descriptive sentences used in the text in Lesson 2.

- Put the class into groups of five with wordcards to make a human sentence:
  - *Il y a neuf planètes.*
  - *Il y a neuf couleurs.*
  - *Saturne est une planète orange.*
  - *Mars est une planète rouge.*
  - *Jupiter est une planète petite.*
  - *De quelle couleur est Jupiter ?*
  Can the class read the sentences aloud?

- Introduce and explain *près de …* and *loin de …*
  Say and write on the whiteboard sentences about children's places in the room. For example: *Sarah est près de Laura. Jack est loin de Laura.* Challenge the children to say a sentence about two classmates.

- Use the qualifiers *assez* and *très*: for example, *Jack est assez près de Matthew.* Can the children tell their talk partner a sentence using *assez*? (Explain that *de* changes to *du* if *le* is going to come next: for example *La porte est loin du pupitre.*)

- Play **Solar system**; individuals taking the roles of the sun and some planets. (Include Mercury and Pluto.) After the human planets have introduced themselves (*Je m'appelle… Venus*) can partners make up a sentence about their positions?

Follow-up
Give the children photocopiable 18B to order the planets and write about their positions.

Lesson 4
Le soleil et les planètes
(The sun and the planets)
Resources
10 PE hoops; a list of sentences provided; an interactive whiteboard (if possible)

- Divide the class into nine groups, allocating each group a planet.

- Stand in a PE hoop at one end of the room with nine PE hoops at intervals on the floor between you and the other end of the room. Announce: *Je m'appelle le soleil.*

- Invite the groups to place themselves in the correct hoop and announce which planet they are. Is every planet in the correct place?

- Say *Le soleil est très, très chaud.* Do the children understand? Can they describe their planet's temperature? (Have a word bank on display.) Can they describe their planet's position in relation to you, the sun? (For example: *La terre est assez près du soleil.*)

- Write this English text on the whiteboard:
  'Mercury is a very hot planet. Mercury is very close to the sun.'
  Ask the children to think of an English conjunction to join the two simple sentences into one compound sentence. Replace the full stop with 'because'.

- Underneath, write the equivalent French compound sentence:
  Mercure est une planète très chaude <u>parce que</u> Mercure est très près du soleil.

- Return to the English version. Ask partners to read it to each other a few times. Which word would they not have repeated? Agree that the second 'Mercury' would usually be replaced by the pronoun 'it'.

- Demonstrate doing the same with the French compound sentence:
  Mercure est une planète très chaude parce qu'<u>elle</u> est très près du soleil.
  Point out the pronoun *elle*, emphasising that it replaces the feminine noun *Mercure*.

- Display separate, simple sentences, preferably on an interactive whiteboard. Let the children work with a partner as they decide which to pair into a compound sentence with *parce que* or *et*. Where will they use a pronoun? Share oral answers and, if using an interactive whiteboard, drag and drop sentences into these pairs, link with *parce que* or *et* and make pronoun substitutions:
  - *La terre est assez chaude. La terre est assez près du soleil. (parce que)*
  - *Le soleil est jaune. Le soleil est très, très chaud. (et)*
  - *Pluton est très froid. Pluton est très loin du soleil. (parce que)*

Follow-up
Set the children the task of creating a booklet or interactive game. The aim must be to provide information and descriptions of important features of a planet. For example: a game could have multiple choice questions; a board could have lift-up flaps, under which are the answers to questions on the flaps. Let the children consider using computers.

1	2	3
4	5	6
7	8	9

Un, deux, trois!

la Terre	Vénus	Mercure
Saturne	Jupiter	Mars
Pluton	Neptune	Uranus

Décrivez les planètes

Uranus
Mars
la Terre
Mercure
Jupiter
Neptune
Saturne

Fill in the missing labels. Check that you have the planets in the correct order.

1. _____ est près du soleil.

2. _____ est loin du soleil.

3. Mercure _____ très chaude.

4. Pluton est une planète _____.

5. Uranus _____

6. Saturne _____

7. La terre _____

Fill in the missing words in the early sentences. Make up your own descriptions in the later sentences.

More ideas for...

Work at school

- Put the children into twos with 18 blank cards. Ask them to put their cards into pairs: on one card they should write the name of a planet; on the other card, an appropriate description. To play **Pelmanism**, the cards are shuffled and spread out, face down. Partners take turns choosing two to turn over: if a description and planet match, the player keeps the cards; if not, the cards are turned back over, in the same spot. The winner is the player with more matching pairs at the end of the game.

- Throughout the week, give the children regular practice in the use of the qualifiers *assez* and *très*: for example, in a science lesson, comment in French as well as English on the temperature of the liquids in the experiment; in a numeracy lesson, comment in French as well as English on the relative distances between the locations and your school.

- Hold a fun games session, in which the children play with other people's packs of cards made in the last activity and the games made in Lesson 4. Reading one another's descriptions and answers will improve the children's French while teaching them about the solar system.

Work at home

- After Lesson 1, give the children photocopiable 18A to take home. Suggest they cut out the cards and play regular games of **Line them up** and **What's my name?** so they become familiar with the planets' names and spelling.

- Having introduced the noun *la lune* (the moon) ask the children to find out three simple facts about the moon. Can they use their information to write two or three descriptive sentences in French about the moon?

- Give the children a vocabulary resource of the names of days of the week. Explain that a day of the week is linked to a planet, the sun or the moon. Can the children recognise or discover which day relates to what and why?

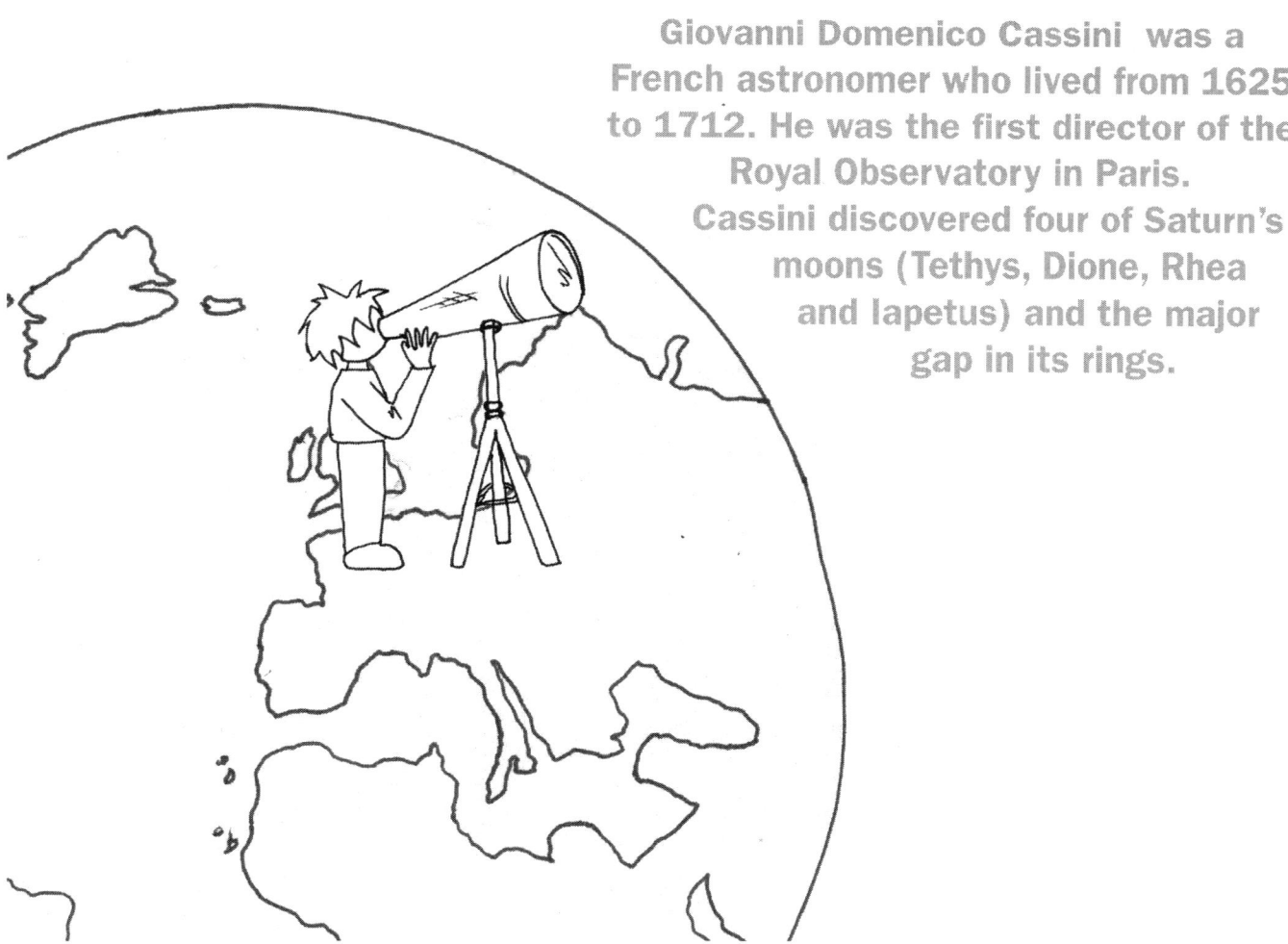

Giovanni Domenico Cassini was a French astronomer who lived from 1625 to 1712. He was the first director of the Royal Observatory in Paris. Cassini discovered four of Saturn's moons (Tethys, Dione, Rhea and Iapetus) and the major gap in its rings.

Unit 19 – Notre école

(Our school)

Unit theme
- School places and routines

Teaching points
- Talking about school routines, subjects and environment
- Reporting breaktime activities, referring to the past
- Telling the time, using half-hours, quarter-hours
- The 24 hour clock notation

Grammar
- Definite and indefinite articles: *le/la; un/une*
- Perfect tense

Language sounds
- *qu*

Vocabulary

Il est midi/minuit	It is midday/midnight
Il est une heure et demie / Il est deux heures et demie, etc	It is half past one / It is half past two, etc
Il est deux heures et quart / Il est deux heures moins le quart	It is a quarter past two / It is a quarter to two
Il est quatorze heures trente	It is 14.30
le terrain de sport	the sports field
la salle de classe	the classroom
la cour	the playground
les toilettes (f plural)	the toilets
la récré	breaktime
J'ai joué	I played
J'ai parlé	I spoke
J'ai dansé	I danced
J'ai aidé	I helped
J'ai travaillé	I worked
J'ai chanté	I sang
le dessin	art
le sport	sport
le français	French
la géographie	geography
la technologie	design and technology
l'anglais (m)	English
l'informatique (f)	ICT
l'histoire (f)	history
les sciences (f plural)	science
les maths (f plural)	maths
C'est l'heure!	It's time!
le parking	the car park
la grande salle	the hall
la bibliothèque	the library
la cuisine	the kitchen
l'entrée (f)	the entrance
Comment ça s'écrit?	How is that spelt?
un emploi du temps	a timetable
le déjeuner	lunchtime
L'école commence à	What time does school start?
C'est quand …?	When is …?
Qu'est-ce que tu as fait (pendant la récré)?	What did you do (at breaktime)?
un copain (m)/*une copine* (f)	a friend
mes copains	(m plural) my friends
mes copines	(f plural)
C'était super!	It was great!

Additional vocabulary for teachers

Où est...?	Where is...?
Fermez/ferme les yeux	Close (plural/singular) your eyes
Ouvrez/ouvre les yeux	Open (plural/singular) your eyes

Un, deux, trois!

Resources
Jacques, the class puppet

Lesson 1 Big Ben
(Big Ben)

Resources
A large teaching clock with movable hands; small teaching clocks for the children to use

- Set a large teaching clock with movable hands to 11 o'clock.

- Write the question *Quelle heure est-il?* on the whiteboard. Do the children understand? Remind them how to say *Il est onze heures.* (See Units 11 and 15).

- Repeat the question about new times on the clock, keeping to the hour or half past the hour.

- Introduce *midi* and *minuit*, explaining that they both mean 12 o'clock.

- Put the children into twos with small clocks. They must take turns controlling the clock, making a time on the hour or half past the hour. When they show their partner the clock and ask *Quelle heure est-il?* can their partner say the time and win a point?

- Remind the children how to write a time digitally: for example 11.30. Give them practice after you have said a time sentence: for example, *Il est dix heures et demie* (10.30).

- Play **Big Ben** by writing in 24 hour digital notation displays on the whiteboard of your clock's future new times (for example, 14.30). For each, ask everyone to secretly set the hands of their individual clock accordingly. Choose two children to set Big Ben. When you all compare results, do most children agree with Big Ben?

- Explain that two buses make journeys between the village centre and school. Ask the children to create an information sheet to send to parents showing:
  - the morning departure times of the two buses from the village, and their arrival times at school;
  - the afternoon departure times from school of the same two buses, and their arrival times in the village.

- Suggest drawing places and presenting time information in three ways: a clock face; digital recording; a written sentence. Provide an example: a drawn clock face, hands placed appropriately; 16.00; *Il est quatre heures.*

Follow-up
Point out that *midi* and *minuit* often cause confusion. Challenge the children, in pairs, to work out a tip to help the class remember which is which. Let them write and illustrate their tip. When you display them, which ones do the class think are good memory prompts?

In French state schools, children do not wear a school uniform.

Lesson 2 Voici l'école (Here is the school)

Resources
Photographs of important places in the school

- Indicate the classroom and say: *Voici la salle de classe.* Using the same *Voici ...* sentence, point out and name these places: *le terrain de sport, la cour, les toilettes.*

- Identify additional places: *le parking, la grande salle, la bibliothèque, la cuisine, l'entrée.*

- Repeat the names as you show the children photographs of the places.

- Turn the pictures over and, in random order, write the names on the whiteboard.

- Set a challenge. Working in pairs, the children must decide which written French name is what place. Encourage deduction, not memory: knowledge of other French vocabulary and similarities between French and English words will help. Provide sentence constructions for French partner discussion: for example, *Je pense que 'la cuisine' est 'the kitchen' en anglais.* (I think that 'la cuisine' is 'the kitchen' in English.) When checking in a dictionary, one partner can ask for the spelling with *Comment ça s'écrit?* The other must reply by spelling out the French letters.

- Share information as a class, the children disclosing how they reached their answers.

- Display the photographs again. Let the class be tour guides: as you point to a picture, they announce it with the sentence *Voici ... (l'entrée).*

- Put the children into pairs with a copy of photocopiable 19A, the cards and words cut out, for these games:
  - **Beat the clock**
    The children spread out their picture cards face up. Having set themselves a time limit, they label the pictures with the words. Do they beat the clock? With the cards placed randomly again, can they beat a new, lower time limit?
  - **Pronunciation points**
    The children take turns reading aloud a label. Their partner, acting as judge, holds up a score card of one, two or three. Who wins more pronunciation points?

- **Pelmanism**
  Picture cards and words are shuffled and spread out face down. Partners take turns revealing two cards. If the cards are a matching picture and label, the player keeps them; if not, they are returned face down to the same places.

Follow-up
Ask the children to draw a map of a tour of the school for prospective pupils and their parents. For each place marked on the map, they should write what they, as tour guide, will say.

Lesson 3 Un emploi du temps (A timetable)

Resources
A large teaching clock with movable hands; small teaching clocks for the children to use

- Use the teaching clock to revise the time work from Lesson 1: set the hands to a time and ask *Quelle heure est il?*

- Set the hands at 11.15 and say *Il est onze heures et quart*; set them at 10.45 and say *Il est onze heures moins le quart.*

- Call out quarter to and quarter past times for the children to make on their individual clocks. Invite individuals to be the caller as you watch the children making the time.

- Put on the whiteboard a timetable of a busy day at school, crammed with subjects! Write the subject names in English and use digital time notation beside them.

- Work through the subject names as you, helped by the children and bilingual dictionaries, translate them into French. (Use an interactive whiteboard, with French subject names already concealed by you.)

- Question the children about the timetable: for example, *Le français, c'est à quelle heure? (C'est à deux heures.)*

- Put the times into 24 hour clock notation and repeat the preceding question for the answer: *C'est à quatorze heures.*

- Divide the class into two or three teams. Suggest team members put themselves into pairs with *oui* and *non* voting cards. (They could write on individual whiteboards.)

- Invite each team in turn to choose a pair to say a sentence about the time of a subject on the timetable. The rest of the class vote whether the statement is true. After five minutes which team has said more true sentences?

Follow-up
Make a recording and play 'The timetable song' to the children:
Lundi j'écris l'anglais,

Un, deux, trois!

Mardi je parle le français,
Mercredi j'écoute la musique.
Jeudi c'est l'histoire et la géographie,
Vendredi c'est super !
J'aime le sport !

Play it a few times, the children listening and beginning to join in. Ask them to list the five days and beside each write that day's subjects in English. When partners compare timetables, have they identified the same subjects? Finally, display the song's words.

Lesson 4 Pendant la récré (At breaktime)

Resources
Timetable from Lesson 3; class puppet

- Introduce the word *hier*. Display a version of yesterday's timetable, in French. Show times and include break *(la récré)* and lunchtime *(le dejeuner)*

- As in Lesson 3, question the children about the times of subjects and breaks. Challenge them to make a statement about the timetable to their talk partner.

- Get out the class puppet, Jacques. Ask him *Qu'est-ce que tu as fait hier récré?* (What did you do yesterday breaktime?) Answer for him: for example, *Pendant la récré, j'ai joué au football.* Mime the action.

- Teach other answers. For example: *j'ai mangé; j'ai chanté, j'ai travaillé, j'ai parlé avec mon ami.*

- Test the children's memories as you say one of the sentences about what you did at breaktime. Can the children mime the action?

- Ask the children to think what they did at breaktime yesterday. Can they tell their talk partner in French? Will their partner mime the correct action?

- With the children, write a timetable for what you did at breaktime each day last week. For example: *Lundi j'ai mangé beaucoup. Mardi j'ai...*

- Read the timetable together as the children perform the actions.

- Put the children into groups of five, each to take one day of last week. Encourage group collaboration as each child writes and practises a sentence stating what they did.

- Watch and listen to each group's human breaktime timetable. Which week was the most fun?

Follow-up
Ask the children to create their own, new breaktime timetable for last week. Discuss formats and suggest the title *La semaine dernière* (Last week). Encourage pictures as well as writing.

In French schools, children are likely to sit at individual desks in rows.

la salle de classe   le terrain de sport   la cour

les toilettes   le parking   la grande salle

la bibliothèque   la cuisine   l'entrée

Qu'est-ce que tu as fait pendant la récré?

For each picture, copy the sentence that says what I did.
You will have to complete some.

J'ai aidé _____
J'ai joué au hockey.
J'ai chanté.
J'ai joué au _____
J'ai _____

J'ai mangé.
J'ai travaillé.
J'ai parlé avec mes copains.
J'ai bu.

More ideas for...

Work at school

- Add reality to this unit's theme by making contact with a partner school in a French-speaking country. (Your local town may be twinned with a town in France.) Set up email contact so the children can inform one another about life in their respective schools. Suggest the schools exchange photographs of their school. Pictures annotated by their French-speaking counterparts will provide the children with an interesting, discussion-provoking classroom display.

- Play **The gender game**. Make a large cardboard dice and label each face *cour; parking; cuisine; déjeuner; récré;* and *bibliothéque*. Roll the dice and invite the children to decide whether the resulting noun is masculine or feminine. Encourage the children to use both the definite and indefinite article each time: for example, *la récré, une récré*.

- Make a new large cardboard dice and label each face either *masculin* or *feminin*. Roll the dice as previously, but this time challenge the children to think of a suitable school noun.

- Extend your work on time by making a display of three clock faces.
  - Draw the hands of the first clock at 10 o'clock and write *Il est dix heures.*
  - Draw the hands of the third clock at 11 o'clock and write *Il est onze heures.*
  - Label the times on the middle clock at five minute intervals: *Il est dix heures cinq /dix/vingt/vingt-cinq. Il est onze heures moins vingt-cinq /vingt/ dix, cinq.* Include half-hours and quarter-hours.

- Give the children a copy of 'The timetable song' from Lesson 3. Ask them to write a second verse, repeating the five days but with new verbs and subjects. Make sure the children have access to a bank of relevant vocabulary and bilingual dictionaries.

Work at home

- Give the children photocopiable 19A. Suggest they improve their French spelling and word recognition by playing the games from Lesson 2 with someone at home.

- Ask the children to draw a plan of their real (or ideal) school. Give them photocopiable 19A to use the vocabulary to label the plan. Are there places and vocabulary they want to add?

- Suggest the children think about what they would like to learn about French school life. Then they could write a set of questions in English to send to a child in a French-speaking school. Point out the need to keep the language of the questions clear and simple.

- Give the children the sentences from photocopiable 19B. Ask them to draw a picture and write the English translation for each.

French schoolchildren have
very long holidays:
117 days a year!

Un, deux, trois!

Unit 20 – Notre monde
(Our world)

Unit theme
- The world

Teaching points
- Identifying and naming continents
- Making statements about rivers of the world
- Forecasting the weather
- Using a non-fiction text

Grammar
- Simple superlatives
- Expressing the immediate future: *aller* + infinitive
- Using pronouns: *il/elle*

Language sounds
- *-ique; -gne*
- Key phonemes

Vocabulary

l'Europe (f)	Europe
l'Afrique (f)	Africa
l'Amérique du Sud (f)	South America
l'Amérique du Nord (f)	North America
l'Asie (f)	Asia
l'Océanie (f)	Australasia
l'Antarctique (f)	Antarctica
le plus grand / la plus grande	the biggest
Il va faire beau, etc	It's going to be fine (weather), etc
Il va pleuvoir	It's going to rain
Il va neiger	It's going to snow
Dans quel continent est l'Amazone?	Which continent is the Amazon in?
L'Amazone est en Amérique du Sud	The Amazon is in South America

L'Amazone (m)	The Amazon
Le Congo	The Congo
Le Danube	The Danube
Le Gange	The Ganges
Le Nil	The Nile
Le Rhin	The Rhine
Le Yang Tsé	The Yangtze
La Seine	The Seine
La Tamise	The Thames
Le fleuve se jette dans la mer / l'océan	The river flows into the sea/ocean
la source	the source
un lac	a lake
un marais	a swamp
un désert	a desert
une chute	a waterfall
une ville	a town
une montagne	a mountain
une forêt tropicale	a rainforest
une vallée	a valley

Additional vocabulary for teachers

Dans quel continent est...?	In which continent is...?
Quel temps va-t-il faire?	What is the weather going to be like?
Pour cette activité, vous êtes explorateurs	For this activity, you are explorers
Notre exploration va commencer en août	Our exploration is going to start in August
On va explorer le...	We're going to explore the...

Resources

A globe, atlases and a world map

Lesson 1
Notre monde fantastique (Our fantastic world)

Resources

A globe; atlases; a world map; unnamed continent outlines

- Use a globe to identify and name the continents: *l'Europe, l'Afrique, l'Amérique du Sud, l'Amérique du Nord, l'Asie, l'Océanie, l'Antarctique.*

- Keep to oral work as the children practise pronunciation of the continent names in **Follow my leader**: you vary the way you say the names (fast/ slowly/quietly/loudly); the children repeat them in the same way.

- Display outline shapes of continents. Challenge the children to name them in French.

- Repeat the names. Ask the children to identify three with the same final sound. (*l'Afrique, l'Amérique du Sud, l'Amérique du Nord*) What is the final sound? (*-ique*)

- Write *-ique* on the whiteboard. Ask the children to memorise the grapheme. Cover it up. Can partners write the grapheme in the air? Can they write it on their mini-whiteboard? Reveal your writing: is everyone correct?

- Ask the children what other words they know ending *–ique*. (*fantastique, la Belgique, magnifique, la musique, comique*)

- Let the children try writing the continents' names before you display the written forms. Do the children think they are getting better at writing French sounds that they hear?

- Explain that rivers of the world are important in this unit. Ask the children to tell their partner two in English. Can they name four between them? Share results.

- Display this list of French names of important world rivers: *l'Amazone; le Congo; le Danube; le Gange; le Nil; le Rhin; le Yang Tsé; la Seine; la Tamise.*

- Point out the masculine and feminine articles and locate the rivers on a globe or atlas: for example, *Voici... le Nil.*

Follow-up

Give the children an unmarked map of the world. Ask them to label its continents and identify three rivers.

Lesson 2 Les fleuves du monde (Rivers of the world)

Resources

A globe; atlases; a world map; unnamed continent outlines

- Revise the names of continents and rivers from Lesson 1:
  - Show or draw in the air the shapes of continents for the children to name.
  - Read through the list of important world rivers together.

- On a world map, identify the Rhone and say *La Rhône est en Europe.* Locate other rivers on the list and help the children construct similar sentences stating their continent.

- Enlarge, display and read aloud Part 1 of photocopiable 20A, pausing regularly so children can point to where you have reached.

- Read the text again. Ask English comprehension questions:
  - Which rivers are mentioned?
  - Which river is talked about most?
  - Can you find one fact given about that river? Encourage partner discussion before you share answers as a class.

- Read the text again as the children follow. Point out facts and names the children have mentioned. Underline *il* in the text (used four times). Can the children work out why *il* is used? (It is a pronoun standing in place of *L'Amazone.* Its use avoids too much repetition of the river's name.)

- Ask *L'Amazone, il est en quel continent?* Invite the children to write the answer on their mini-whiteboard. Compare results. Accept *L'Amazone est en Amérique du Sud* but encourage *Il est en Amerique du Sud.*

- Ask the same question about the Thames: *La Tamise, elle est en quel continent?* Point out *elle* (not *il*) because *La Tamise* is feminine. Ask the children to answer with a pronoun (*Elle est en Europe.*)

Follow-up

Put the children into pairs to question and answer each other about the rivers and the continents they are in. Remind them to be careful to use the correct pronoun. After oral practice, they should each write three questions and their answers, using pronouns.

Lesson 3 Quel temps va-t-il faire? (What is the weather going to be like?)

Resources
Weather symbols; a globe; a world map; six large, cardboard cubes with weather symbols on the faces

- Display and read aloud the text from Lesson 2.

- Explain that you want to extract the important information in French from the text. Give the children a facts chart made up of two columns. In the first column, have these headings: *1. Nom du fleuve 2. La longueur 3. Sa source 4. L'embouchure 5. Autres informations.*

- Ask partners to work out what the headings mean before agreeing as a class. (1. Name of the river 2. Length 3. Source 4. Mouth of river 5. Other information).

- Ask the partners to fill in the second column in French about the Amazon by reading the text carefully. Check answers as a class. What *Autres informations* was picked out?

- Make a display of weather symbols, point to one and ask *Quel temps fait-il?* Let partners give each other an answer before you accept an answer from the class.

- Say and write this question: *Quel temps va-t-il faire demain?* (What is the weather going to be like tomorrow?) Point out that the question is about the future and is expressed by the verb *aller* (va) with an infinitive (faire).

- Let the children become weather forecasters and answer your question with *Il va...*

- Make the children form a large circle around you. Use a large dice, a weather symbol on each face. Ask about the future weather somewhere on the globe, for example: *Quel temps va-t-il faire en Angleterre?* Toss the cube: whoever catches it must forecast the weather on the top face. (For example: *En Angleterre il va faire du brouillard.*)

- Make more cubes and divide the class into groups of six for the children to play the game. Make sure that everyone makes a forecast.

Follow-up
Give the children photocopiable 20B. Explain that the female explorer is going to follow the course of a river. She wants to know what the weather will be like in these places when she is there.

Lesson 4 On va explorer (We're going to explore)

Resources
Photocopiable 20B; the children's work from the **Follow-up** Lesson 3

- Return the children's weather forecasts (photocopiable 20B, **Follow-up** Lesson 3) and let some children read theirs out.

- Explain that the features on photocopiable 20B are all likely scenery at stages of a river's journey. Have the children other scenery suggestions (in English) to add?

- Share ideas and write on the whiteboard *un lac, un desert, une chute, la mer, l'océan.* Suggest adding these features' pictures or symbols to photocopiable 20B.

- Invite the children to join you on a journey tracking your imaginary river. Announce *On va explorer le Zukoro.* (We're going to explore the Zukoro.) The children must help you write about the start of the journey along your imaginary river.

- Write a text together. Make sure you keep using the river's name. For example:
  - *On va explorer le Zukoro. Le Zukoro est en Asie. Le Zukoro est le plus long fleuve d'Asie. Le Zukoro est long de 5,500km. La source du Zukoro est en Pakistan dans les montagnes. Le Zukoro traverse les vallées. En août dans les vallées il va faire du vent.* (We are going to explore the Zukoro. The Zukoro is in Asia. The Zukoro is the longest river in Asia. The Zukoro is 5,500km long. The source of the Zukoro is in Pakistan in the mountains. In August in the mountains it's going to be windy.)

- Read your text together. Do the children notice the name's repetition? What would be better? (Some use of the pronoun *il*.) Make these changes and save this model text.

- Put the children into pairs to map the route of their own imaginary river. Suggest showing their river's course on a poster; in separate pictures; or in a power point presentation

- Partners will make an oral presentation to an audience, so they must prepare a written sentence for each stage of the river's journey.

- Let the children practise before they make their presentation to others.

Follow-up
Explain that the children, as explorers, will make a journey of four or five months as they explore the track of their imaginary river. Using the class model text as an example and still in pairs, they must write a similar paragraph about any month and stage of their planned journey.

Les fleuves du monde

En chaque continent il y a un grand fleuve. Le Rhône est en Europe. Il y a le Nil en Afrique. En Amérique du Sud il y a l'Amazone. Il est le plus grand fleuve d'Amérique du Sud. Il est le deuxième plus grand du monde après le Nil. L'Amazone est long de 6,440km. Sa source est en Pérou dans les montagnes des Andes. Il traverse le Brésil et il se jette finalement dans l'Océan Atlantique.

- -

PART 2

Each continent has a big river. The Rhône is in Europe. There is the Nile in Africa. In South America there is the Amazon. It is the second-biggest river in the world after the Nile. The Amazon is 6,440km long. Its source is in the Andes Mountains. It flows through Brazil. Finally, it flows out into the Atlantic Ocean.

- -

Nom du fleuve	
La longueur	
Sa source	
L'embouchure	
Autres informations	

Quel temps va-t-il faire ?

Weather phrases:

Il va...

faire du soleil   pleuvoir

faire chaud   faire mauvais

faire froid   neiger

faire du vent

Give the river explorer a written forecast for each month. For example:

En juillet dans les montagnes il va faire froid.

juillet *les montagnes*	**août** *les hauts plateaux*	**septembre** *la forêt tropicale*

octobre *les vallées*	**novembre** *une ville*	**décembre** *les marais*
	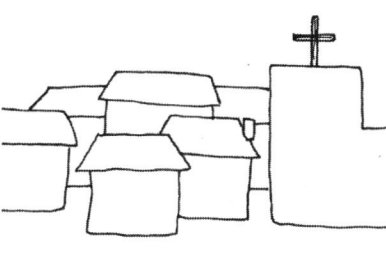	

Un, deux, trois!

Photocopiable 20B

57

More ideas for...

Work at school

- After the children have done the English comprehension questions in the first 'Work at home' activity, give them a copy of that text (see 'Work at home', Activity 1), 'La Tamise' and Part 3 of photocopiable 20A so they can complete the facts table (in French) about the text.

- Create a weather corner, with the headings **Aujourd'hui** (Today) and **Demain** (Tomorrow). Choose a different pair of children each day to:
  - select a weather symbol and write a weather report of today's weather (in present tense);
  - select a weather symbol and write a weather forecast for tomorrow's weather (immediate future tense, using *aller* + infinitive).

- Refer to the children's presentation in Lesson 4 and their written work in the '**Follow-up**'. Ask them to write a similar text about a different month and stage as they explore the track of their imaginary river.

Work at home

- Write and give the children a copy of this text:
  La Tamise
  La Tamise est un fleuve très important en Angleterre. Elle est longue de 338km. Sa source est près de Cirencester et elle se jette finalement dans la mer du Nord. Elle traverse Londres, la capitale de l'Angleterre.

  Set the children these comprehension questions to answer in English:
  a. Which river is talked about?
  b. What country is it in?
  c. Where is the river's source?
  d. Does the river go near London?
  e. Can you find one other fact given about the river?

- Ask the children to write a translation of the text used in the previous activity.
  (The Thames is a very important river in England. It is 338km long. Its source is near Cirencester and finally it flows into the North Sea. It runs through London, the capital of England.)

- Ask the children to find six rivers in France. Can they write their names in French and English?

The River Seine runs through the centre of Paris. Boat trips on the Seine give tourists a good view of many famous buildings.

Un, deux, trois!

Unit 21 Monter un café

(Creating a café)

Unit theme
- Food and drinks

Teaching points
- Food and drink quantities
- Making a café transaction
- Checking the meaning

Grammar
- Perfect verb tense: third person singular (*il/elle a mangé; il/elle a bu*)
- Prepositions: *au, à la*

Language sounds
- Using phoneme-grapheme correspondence to work out the pronunciation of words phonemes
- *-ill-*

Vocabulary

un coca	a cola
un milkshake	a milkshake
un chocolat chaud	a hot chocolate
un café	a (black) coffee
un café au lait	a coffee with milk
un paquet de chips	a packet of crisps
une limonade	a lemonade
une eau minérale	a mineral water
une tasse de thé	a cup of tea
une portion de frites	a portion of chips
une pizza	a pizza
Il/elle a mangé	He/she ate
Il/elle a bu	He/she drank
une glace au chocolat / à la fraise / à la vanille	a chocolate/strawberry/ vanilla ice cream
Je ne comprends pas	I don't understand
Répétez, s'il vous plaît	Can you repeat please? (polite form)

un croque-monsieur	a toasted cheese and ham sandwich
un croque-madame	a toasted cheese, ham and egg sandwich
une salade niçoise	a tuna and egg salad
un diabolo menthe	a mint cordial with lemonade
des moules-frites	mussels and chips
au fromage	with cheese
au thon	with tuna
au pâté	with pâté
au jambon	with ham
une glace au cassis/ au citron/au caramel/ à la framboise/à la pistache/à la menthe/ à l'abricot	a blackcurrant/lemon/ toffee/raspberry/pistachio/ mint/ apricot ice cream
Une boule/ deux boules/ trois boules	One scoop/two scoops/ three scoops

Additional language for teachers

Qu'est-ce que tu as mangé/ bu hier?	What did you eat/drink yesterday?
Qu'est-ce qu'il/elle a mangé/ bu hier?	What did he/she eat/drink yesterday?
Qu'est-ce qu'il y a au menu?	What is on the menu?
les snacks	(m) the snacks
les boissons	(f) the drinks
les glaces	(f) the ice creams
un verre	a glass
un litre	a litre
une cuillère à soupe	a soup spoon
une cuillère à café	a teaspoon
selon le goût	according to taste
Dégustez froid	Eat or drink chilled
En anglais on dit...	In English we say...

Resources
Pictures of French cafés

Lesson 1 Le menu (The menu)

Resources
A picture of a typical French café; individual copies of photocopiable 21A, Part 1; an enlarged copy of photocopiable 21A, Part 1

- Display a picture of a typical French café. In English, ask: What sort of place is this? Have you been to a French café? What was it like? Did it differ from English cafés?

- Display an enlarged copy of Part 1, photocopiable 21A. Explain that the words and prices are from a French café's menu.

- Put the children into pairs with a copy of Part 1, photocopiable 21A. Ask them to mark the words with three colours to represent:
  - words they know;
  - words they can probably guess;
  - words they do not know.

- As a class, compare results and strategies used to guess meanings.

- Make a list on the whiteboard of unknown words (without saying them). Put the children into pairs with a dictionary. Challenge them to find and write the meanings quickly. Can they use their existing knowledge of phoneme-grapheme correspondence to work out how to pronounce the new words?

- Share ideas and help the children with correct pronunciation.

- Bring out Jacques, the class puppet. He always chooses lunch from this café's menu!

- Using the perfect tense (see Unit 13) ask him *Qu'est-ce que tu as mangé hier?* Through you, let him answer in the perfect tense: for example, *J'ai mangé une pizza.*

- Let the class ask the same question of you, your Teaching Assistant or an individual child. The person answering must say aloud *J'ai mangé* but only mouth the actual food. Will the class be able to identify the food?

- Play the game in pairs: one partner asking, the other saying and mouthing a reply. After three questions and answers, how many children identified all three mouthed foods? Did the speaker say the perfect tense correctly?

Follow-up
Supply these headings: *Les sandwichs* (Sandwiches); *Les snacks* (Snacks); *Les glaces* (Ice cream); *Les boissons froids* (Cold drinks); *Les boissons chauds* (Hot drinks). Suggest the children sort and write the menu in these sections. Will the customer need any pictures?

Lesson 2 Qu'est-ce que tu as mangé hier? (What did you eat yesterday?)

Resources
An enlarged copy of photocopiable 21A, Part 1

- Display the café menu (Lesson 1) suggesting the children ate here yesterday.

- Pose a question in the perfect tense: *Qu'est-ce que tu as mangé hier?* Let the children give an answer to a partner before you accept any. Write a correct answer on the whiteboard. For example: *J'ai mangé un sandwich au fromage.*

- Demonstrate the third person singular form of the perfect tense by saying: *Il a mangé un sandwich* about a boy; *Elle a mangé un sandwich* about a girl.

- Introduce the question *Qu'est-ce que tu as bu hier?*; the children practising *J'ai bu…* and *Il/Elle a bu…*

- Play **Trick or truth**:
  - Ask everyone to draw secretly on their mini-whiteboard something they ate or drank yesterday. Give everyone two voting cards: 'trick' and 'truth'.
  - When it is someone's turn to speak, they say an ate or drank sentence: for example, *J'ai mangé une salade verte.*
  - The class votes on whether the person is saying the item they have drawn.
  - Count the votes, ask the person to show their picture and the class to state what is revealed: for example, *Il a mangé une portion de frites!*
  - If most votes were wrong, the boy wins a **Trick or truth** star.
  - Continue the game, moving between boy and girl speakers and using *J'ai mangé/bu* and *Il/Elle a mangé/bu*.

- You and your Teaching Assistant take the roles of customer and ice cream seller. Encourage the children to help you with dialogue. Include:
  A: *Bonjour monsieur.*
  B: *Bonjour…, vous désirez?*
  A : *Je voudrais une glace…*
  B : *Quel parfum ? J'ai des glaces au chocolat, à la…*
  A: *Une glace…*
  A: *C'est combien?*
  B : *…*

Un, deux, trois!

- Write an agreed dialogue on the whiteboard for the children, to practise, in pairs

Follow-up
On one side of the whiteboard (preferably, an interactive whiteboard) draw four people named Pierre, Nicole, Claude and Claire. On the other side, draw or write food and drinks. In the middle write *a mangé* and *a bu*. Ask the children to mix and match the people, verbs and foods to write sentences about who had what to eat or drink.

Lesson 3 Bon appétit! (Enjoy your food!)

Resources
Cartons of ice cream; milk; sugar; powder flavouring; measuring jugs; mixing bowls; large glasses

- Read out the ingredients for a strawberry milkshake: *25cl de lait* (25 cl of milk); *2 cuillères à soupe de fraises en poudre* (2 soup spoons of strawberry powder); *2 cuillères à café de sucre en poudre (2 teaspoons of sugar powder); *2 boules de glace à la vanille* (2 scoops of vanilla ice cream).

- Say instructions as you mime making the drink: *Mélangez le lait, les fraises et la glace et puis ajoutez le sucre. (*Mix the milk, the strawberries and the ice cream and then add the sugar.)

- Repeat the instructions for the children to mime the actions.

- List new words on the whiteboard. Explain the meaning of *lait* with this sentence: *En anglais on dit 'milk' mais en francais on dit 'lait'.* (In English we say 'milk' but in French we say 'lait'.) Repeat this format for other ingredients and utensils, giving the children time to find the word listed and finish the sentence for you.

- Explain that the children are going to run a milkshake stall! Divide the class into groups. Have a range of ingredients and flavours available, groups deciding which one flavour milkshake to make on their stall. Encourage variety among the class. (Alternatively, let every group run an ice cream stall, on which they display the ice cream cone or wafer they have put together and have taster amounts available.)

- Set out the ingredients for children to take, measure, mix and make.

- Suggest that groups give their drink a name, for example *Chocolat Surprise.*

- Have taster straws available so the children can sip

a few milkshakes, recording their written opinion of each. (For example, *Chocolat Surprise, c'est excellent!*)

- Compare verdicts and ask the children to award drinks a score. Which stall was best?

Follow-up
Suggest the children create a poster to advertise their stall's products. Remind them to mention flavours and prices.

Lesson 4 Un café bizarre (A strange café)

Resources
Individual copies of photocopiable 21B

- Give the children a copy of photocopiable 21B.

- Read through the playscript as the children follow.

- Discuss the meaning of the text. Ask the children: Why is the café strange? What does the waiter keep doing? Why is the customer surprised by the bill?

- Ask the children to identify an example of the perfect tense. (*J'ai commandé*).

- Model reading and acting the play with your Teaching Assistant.

- Divide the class in half, perhaps boys and girls. Allocate the part of waiter to one half, the customer to the other.

- Let the class read the play, the children keeping to their parts. Encourage careful pronunciation and expressive voices and body language.

- Put the class into pairs to read the play. Let the class listen to and watch some performances.

- Suggest that this café and its waiter will go on being strange! Ask what changes could occur in a new script. (Different food, a different customer, different bill total).

- Ask the children, in pairs, to write a new script. Suggest they use photocopiable 21B as a model.

- Allow time for the children to practise reading and acting their play.

Follow-up
Let the children read and perform their plays for other members of the class.

Le menu

Part 1
Words:

Coca 2,00 €

Milkshake 5,00 €

Café au lait 3,00 €

Paquet de chips 1,50 €

Limonade 2,00 €

Eau minérale 2,50 €

Tasse de thé 3,00 €

Portion de frites 3,50 €

au chocolat / à la fraise /
à la vanille

Croque-monsieur 6,00 €

Croque-madame 6,50 €

Orange pressée 3,00 €

Diabolo menthe 2,00 €

Moules-frites 8,50 €

au cassis / au citron / au caramel /
à la framboise / à la pistache /
à l'abricot

Pizza 7,00 €

Chocolat chaud 3,00 €

Café 1,50 €

au fromage 7,00 €

au thon 7,00 €

au pâté 8,00 €

au jambon 7,50 €

Une boule 1,50 €

Deux boules 3,00 €

Trois boules 4,00 €

Citron pressé 3,00 €

- -

Part 2
Likely grouping of words:

Les sandwichs	**Les glaces**	**Les boissons froides**
fromage	au chocolat / au cassis / au caramel /	Eau minérale
au jambon	à la framboise /à la fraise / à l'abricot	Coca
au pâté	/ à la vanille / à la pistache	Milkshake
au thon	Une boule	Limonade
	Deux boules	Diabolo menthe
Les snacks	Trois boules	Citron pressé
Moules-frites		Orange pressée
Croque-monsieur	**Les boissons chaudes**	
Croque-madame	Thé	
Pizza	Café	
Paquet de chips	Café au lait	
Portion de frites	Chocolat chaud	

Le café bizarre

LE SERVEUR: *Bonjour Mademoiselle.*

LA FILLE: *Bonjour Monsieur. Le menu s'il vous plaît.*

LE SERVEUR: *Voilà. Vous désirez?*

LA FILLE: *Je voudrais un café au lait, un sandwich au jambon, une portion de frites et une glace au chocolat.*

LE SERVEUR: *Voilà un café au jambon, un sandwich au café, une portion de chocolat et une glace aux frites.*

LA FILLE: *Non! Non! J'ai commandé un café au lait, un sandwich au jambon, une portion de frites et une glace au chocolat.*

LE SERVEUR: *Oui Mademoiselle. Voilà un café au jambon, un sandwich au café, une portion de chocolat et une glace aux frites.*

LA FILLE: *Berk, c'est combien?*

LE SERVEUR: *Soixante euros!*

LA FILLE: *Soixante euros? C'est un café bizarre!*

- -

The strange café

WAITER: *Hello, miss.*

GIRL: *Hello, sir. The menu please.*

WAITER: *Here you are. What would you like?*

GIRL: *I'd like a coffee with milk, a ham sandwich, a portion of chips and a chocolate ice cream.*

WAITER: *Here you are: a ham coffee, a coffee sandwich, a portion of chocolate and a chips ice cream.*

GIRL: *No! No! I ordered a coffee with milk, a ham sandwich, a portion of chips and a chocolate ice cream.*

WAITER: *Yes, miss. Here you are: a ham coffee, a coffee sandwich, a portion of chocolate and a chips ice cream.*

GIRL: *Yuck, how much is it?*

WAITER: *Sixty euros!*

GIRL: *Sixty euros? This is a strange café!*

More ideas for...

Work at school

- Display a map of France and point out its division into regions. Identify some regions: for example, Provence, Aquitaine, Alsace, Brittany. Ask the children to use the Internet to find out about food popular in each region.

- Extend the customer/seller dialogue in Lesson 2 to include strategies for dealing with situations when you do not understand what is being said. Suggest the use of *Je ne comprends pas* (I don't understand) and *Répétez, s'il vous plâit* (Will you repeat that please?) Let the children try them out in an adapted version of the paired dialogue.

- Set up a café board in your French corner of the classroom. Write on it a changing, short menu of today's foods and drinks. Include new words and encourage partners to read them to each other. Can the children use their knowledge of phoneme-grapheme correspondence to work out the words' pronunciation. Are there clues to their meanings?

Work at home

- Give the children Part 1 of photocopiable 21A. Suggest they use it use it to help them write a bilingual menu (French on one half, English on the other) for their own new café. What special foods will they have? Will their prices be sensible? How tempting will their menu look?

- Ask the children to find out about euros. When was this currency introduced? Which countries use it? Is it worth more or less than the English pound?

- Suggest the children draw a food map of France. They should have regions marked in different colours. Each region should have a picture or name of a food or drink popular in that area.

- Give the children a copy of the dialogue in Lesson 2, between a customer and the ice cream seller. Ask the children to use it as a model as they write their own dialogue between the café owner and a customer as the customer orders something to eat or drink.

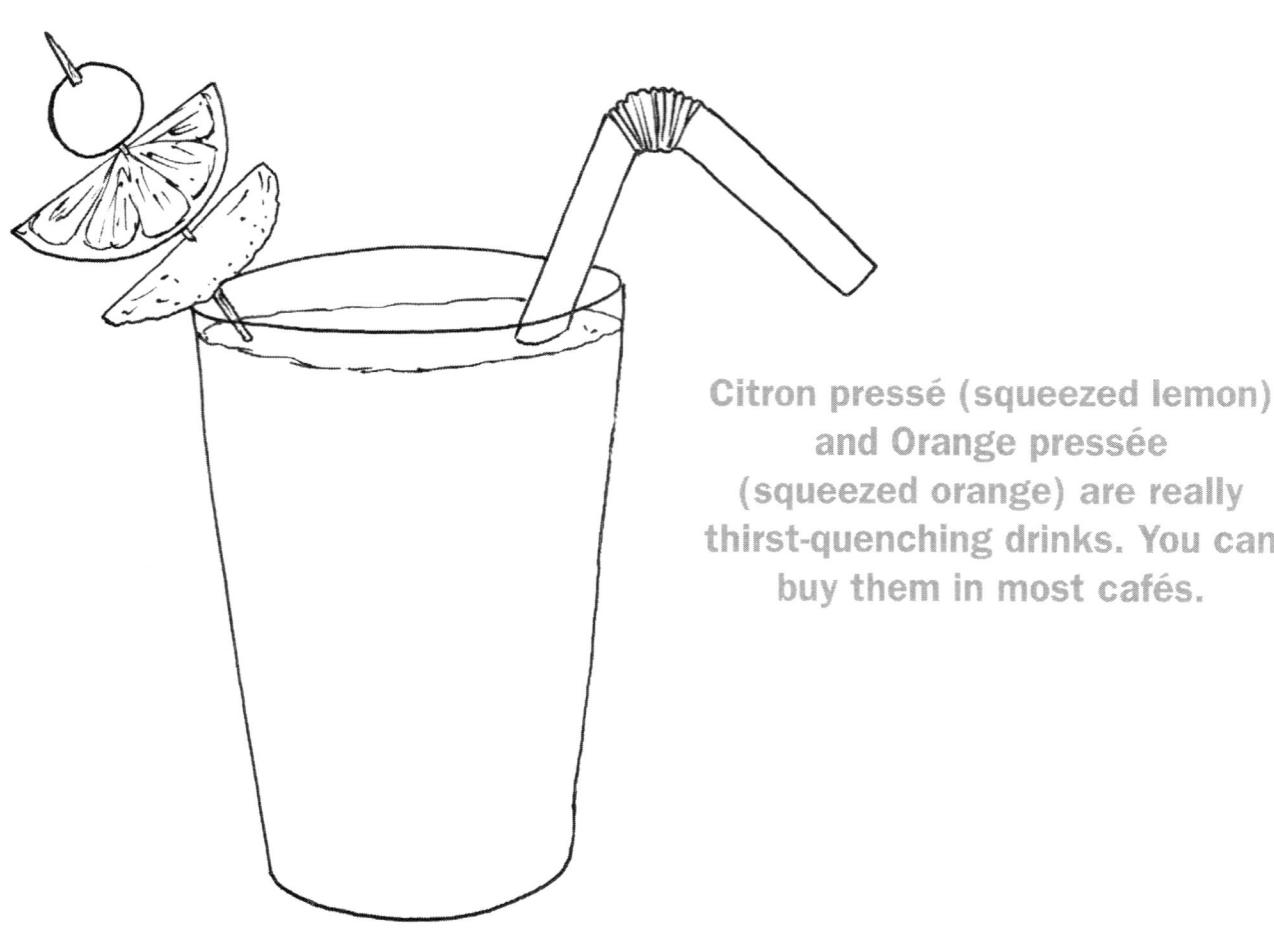

Citron pressé (squeezed lemon) and Orange pressée (squeezed orange) are really thirst-quenching drinks. You can buy them in most cafés.

Un, deux, trois!

Unit 22 –
Le passé et le présent
(Then and now)

Unit theme
- Towns - then and now

Teaching points
- Describing a town

- Comparing a settlement today with one in the past

- Writing a guide for tourists

Grammar
- Antonyms

- Imperfect verb tense of *être (était)* and *avoir (avait)*

- *Beaucoup de...* • *Peu de...*

Language sounds
- *ait*

Vocabulary

le/un supermarché	the/a supermarket
la/une charcuterie	the/a delicatessen (meat)
la/une boulangerie	the/a bakery
la/une boucherie	the/a butcher's
la/une pâtisserie	the/a cake shop
la/une poissonnerie	the/a fishmonger

l'/une épicerie	the/a grocer's
Il y avait...	There was...
C'était...	It was...
aujourd'hui	today
soixante-et-onze, soixante-douze, soixante-treize, etc	71, 72, 73, etc
quatre-vingt-un, quatre-vingt-deux, quatre-vingt-trois, etc	81, 82, 83, etc
quatre-vingt-onze, quatre-vingt-douze, quatre-vingt-treize, etc	91, 92, 93, etc
mille	thousand
beaucoup de	a lot (of)
peu de	few
animé(e)	lively (m/f)
calme	calm
beau/belle	beautiful (m/f)
moderne	modern
vieux/vieille	old (m/f)
moche	ugly

Additional vocabulary for teachers

Il n'y avait pas de...	There wasn't/weren't any...
Il/elle est né(e) en	He/she was born in...

Resources
Photographs or pictures of places in your local town.

Lesson 1 On va visiter un ville (We are going to visit a town)
Resources
Recognisable symbols of familiar town places; a prepared list of places in and absent from local town

- Display recognisable symbols for familiar town places: a shop, cafe, market, railway station, post office and a library. Agree in English what the places are.

- On the whiteboard, write the first letter of each equivalent French noun (*un café, un magasin, une poste, un marché, une gare, une bibliothèque*) but only dashes for the other letters: for example: *un m——; un c–*.

- Tell the children that this is a memory test: these are words they should know!

- Challenge them to remember three of the words, silently list them, and compare results with a partner. Can they remember five or six of the words between them?

- Share results as a class and write the missing letters on the whiteboard.

- Hold up a symbol and ask, for example, *C'est un café?* for a child to answer *Oui, C'est un café* or *Non, c'est un/e…*

- As you question children and they answer, encourage the class to listen carefully. Can they distinguish between your intonation (a question) and the child's (a statement)?

- Play **Up or down?** Pick up a place symbol and ask the class *C'est un marché?* However, make your intonation the flat intonation of a statement. The class should refuse to answer you! They should only answer your questions when your intonation correctly rises. How many children get caught answering at the wrong time? Let individual children take your place at trying to catch the class out.

- Apply the place vocabulary to your local town and say and write a sentence: for example, *À Warwick, il y a un marché.* What sentence can the children work out?

- Draw four places on the whiteboard, ticks next to three, a cross by the fourth. Write a statement: for example *À Warwick, il y a un marché, un café et une musée mais il n'y a pas de boulangerie.* (In Warwick, there is a market, a cafe and a museum, but there is no bakery.) Point out the negative. Leave this on the whiteboard.

- Play **Tourist trail**: two children (tourists) leave the room; the rest of the class agree on three places for their imaginary town; when the tourists return to the room, they try to identify the places, asking for example: *Il y a une musée?* The townspeople chorus a reply. Limit the number of questions allowed (perhaps six). How many places will the tourists identify?

Follow-up
Return to the long statement about Warwick (*À Warwick, il y a… de boulangerie*). Remind the children about the negative. Draw new sets of symbols on the board with three ticks and a cross for the children to create new long statements.

Lesson 2 Le passé et le présent (Then and now)

Resources
Six small foam balls; a current picture of a town and a picture of the same town in about 1948

- Revise numbers, the class counting up to 39. Play **Toss a ten**, the children, in circles of five with a ball: one group member says 10 and throws the ball; the catcher says the next multiple of 10. Can they reach 100? Can they play the game backwards?

- Display this calculation: *60 + 13 = 73*. Underneath, write and explain the French words: *soixante+ treize = soixante-treize.* Challenge the children to say and solve this word calculation: *soixante+ dix-neuf = ? (soixante-dix-neuf).*

- Write on the whiteboard 1948. Ask the children, in pairs, to decide how to say the year in French (*mille dix-neuf cent quarante-huit*). Let them try 1965 (*mille dix-neuf cent soixante-cinq*).

- Write on the board *deux mille dix.* Can the children work out the year? (2010) Point out that *mille* is used instead of *cent* once the date passes 2000.

- Remind the children that this Unit is about past and present towns. Display two pictures: a town in about 1948 and the same town in the present time. Above one picture write, for example, *En 1948*; above the other, *Aujourd'hui.*

- Concentrate on the modern scene, using sentences such as: *Il y trois supermarchés. Il y a une boucherie.* Write the sentences on the whiteboard. Ask what the sentences have in common. (*Il y a*) What does the phrase mean? (There is/are).

- Move to the picture of the past. Explain that *Il y a* must now become *Il y avait.* Can the children guess what it means? (There was/were).

Follow-up
Display these statements. Ask the children to copy them, each time adding a statement about the town today. Afterwards, they must decide how to link each pair: with *et (and)* or *mais (but)*. For example: *En 1948, il y avait une boucherie mais aujourd'hui, il y a un supermarché.*

1. *En 1948, il y avait une boucherie.*
2. *En 1948, il y avait une poissonnerie.*
3. *En 1948, il y avait une petite église.*
4. *En 1948, il y avait une petite école.*
5. *En 1948, il y avait une gare.*

Un, deux, trois!

Lesson 3 Salut! (Hello)

Resources

Individual copies of Part 1, photocopiable 22A and one enlarged copy; a slide show of images for your interactive whiteboard, or drawn pictures for the whiteboard (for **Follow-up**)

- Tell the children that you have found – on a French Internet website - a description of people's local town.

- Give the children a copy of the text (Part 1 of photocopiable 22A). Put them into pairs to try to make sense of the text. Advise they:
  1. highlight words/phrases they know;
  2. read parts aloud.

- Let pairs double up to pool ideas and share findings.

- Display on the whiteboard an enlarged copy of the text, reading it aloud as the children follow. Question them about meaning. What was easy to understand? Why?

- Agree that the text describes the town in the present and in the past. The first paragraph has the present tense verbs a and est. (Il y a... and c'**est**). What are the past tense verbs in the second paragraph? (**avait** and **était**).

- Did the children identify and understand many adjectives in the text? Ask children to come to the whiteboard and identify an adjective. Highlight some of them: grande; animée; nouvelle; utile; vieille; moderne. What is noticeable about the highlighted adjectives? (They all end in e.)

- Write this sentence from the text: C'est aussi une ville très animée. Add this sentence: Le parc est assez animé. Can the children explain why animée loses an e in the second sentence? (Le parc is masculine: la ville is feminine.)

- Work through all the adjectives in the text, giving partners time to confer before you agree on the spelling and pronunciation of their singular masculine and feminine forms (grand/grande; nouveau/nouvelle; utile/utile; vieux/vieille; différent/différente; petit/petite; tranquille/tranquille; moderne/moderne).

- Agree on a mime for each of the preceding adjectives. Play two games:
  1. **Synonyms** When you call out an adjective, the children mime the appropriate action.
  2. **Antonyms** When you call out an adjective, the children mime the opposite. Can anyone say the French opposite?

Follow-up

Give the children, in pairs, a jumbled bank of about 20 adjectives to agree on their meanings and action mimes. In a partner game of **Antonyms**, who scores best at miming the opposite action? What about saying the antonym?

Lesson 4 Les touristes (The tourists)

Resources

An enlarged copy of Part 1, photocopiable 22A; individual copies of photocopiable 22B; a current picture of your town and one taken in about 1948

- Remind the children about the French town information (Part 1, photocopiable 22A).

- Display and investigate the text in more detail. Help the children identify places mentioned.

- Point out important sentence constructions, phrases and adjectives (See Lesson 3).

- Highlight and explain beaucoup de and peu de in the text. Create a slide show of images for your interactive whiteboard, or draw paired pictures on the whiteboard. For each, ask the children to decide which phrase to use: for example, the picture of a big bunch of bananas needs the sentence Il y a beaucoup de bananes; the picture of only a few bananas, Il y a peu de bananes.

- Tell the children your idea: a tourist information leaflet about their town! Display past and present pictures of the town. Discuss paper leaflets and an on-screen version for the school website.

- Give the children photocopiable 22B to write their word bank and notes as they plan their leaflet.

- Encourage the children to show their plans to someone else and ask for comments. (If children prefer to work with a partner, they could ask another pair for feedback.)

- Suggest the children follow the three-step writing routine: 1. Plan 2. Do 3. Review.

- After planning, they do their written draft. They exchange with someone else and receive their comments before they review and re-write their text and create a leaflet with illustrations – by hand or on computer with publishing software.

Follow-up

Let the children pretend to be tourists and read one another's leaflets. Encourage positive feedback as they tell one another what they particularly enjoyed. What made them enthusiastic about exploring the town?

Salut! On Te vous présente notre ville.

Le présent

Aujourd'hui... c'est une ville très grande. C'est aussi une ville très animée. Il y a beaucoup de gens, de magasins et de voitures. Il y a des restaurants, des cafés et quatre supermarchés! Il y a une nouvelle bibliothèque et beaucoup de maisons et appartements modernes. La bibliothèque est très utile. Il y a aussi un parc. Le parc est assez animé. Notre école (qui est vieille) est à coté du parc.

Le passé

En 1948... la ville était très différente. C'était plus petite et c'était moins animée. Il y avait peu de voitures donc le centre-ville était plus tranquille. Il y avait beaucoup de petits magasins – une boucherie, une épicerie et quatre boulangeries! Il n'y avait pas de restaurant mais il y avait deux cafés. En 1948, notre école était moderne!

- -

Hello! Let us present our town to you.

Now

Today... it is a very large town. It is also a very busy town. There are many people, shops and cars. There are restaurants, cafés and four supermarkets! There is a new library and many modern houses and flats. The library is very useful. There is also a park. The park is quite busy. Our school (which is old) is next to the park.

Then

In 1948 the town was very different. It was smaller and less busy. There were few cars so the town centre was more peaceful. There were many small shops – a butcher's, a grocer's, and four bakeries! There was no restaurant but there were two cafés. In 1948, our school was modern!

Le plan

Vocabulary

Places

Adjectives

Important verbs and phrases

Contents

Proposed illustrations

Opening words

More ideas for...

Work at school

- Make this unit an opportunity to establish or reinforce links with a school in a French-speaking country. The children will be able to exchange information about their towns and gain further insight into French life and culture.

- Reinforce the distinction between the speech intonation of a statement and a question by playing games of **Simon dit** ('Simon says'). The children mime the action said only if they hear a statement; they do nothing if they hear a question. For example, *Ouvrez la bouche!* (Open your mouth!) produces a mime; *Ouvrez la bouche?* (Open your mouth?) produces nothing.

- Ask the children to design a symbol for each of the individual shops likely to be in a town of the past or present. Suggest that the symbol should be easily identifiable. The children could provide a key at the bottom of the page.

- Put the children into small groups. Assign a French shop to each group to create shop windows for a class mural. Agree on shop order and numbering, *soixante-treize* onwards. When the display is complete, use it for oral number practice, asking questions such as *La poissonnerie, quel numéro est?* (What number is the fishmonger?)

Work at home

- Give the children a list of French shops and town buildings. Ask the children to match them with the jumbled English list.

- Give the children a copy of Part 1, photocopiable 22A. Suggest they are being paid to translate the text into English. How well can they do?

- Set spelling homework with a difference, choosing vocabulary linked to this Unit. Give the children a list of French shops to learn the gender and spelling. Advise them to use the **Look, Say, Cover, Write, Check** method.

You will probably find a weekly market in any town you visit in France, a good place to buy fresh food. It is common for the market stallholders to let you try some of the food they are selling.

Un, deux, trois!

Unit 23
Au parc d'attractions
(At the theme park)

Unit theme
- The theme park

Teaching points
- Talking about a visit to a theme park, referring to the past

- Using adjectives to add detail and interest

- Expressing an opinion

Grammar
- Perfect verb tense with *être*: *aller (je suis allé (m); je suis allée (f))*

- Perfect verb tense with *avoir*: *prendre (j'ai pris); voir (j'ai vu); entendre (j'ai entendu)*

Language sounds
- *u*

Vocabulary

un parc d'attractions	a theme park
passionnant	exciting
terrifiant	frightening
rapide	fast
sensationnel	amazing
marrant	funny
merveilleux	marvellous
énorme	enormous
fantastique	fantastic
génial	great
Je suis allé (m); *Je suis allée*	(f) I went

J'ai pris le train fantôme	I went for a ride on the ghost train
J'ai vu...	I saw...
J'ai entendu...	I heard...
le grand huit	the rollercoaster
le carrousel	the merry-go-round
le train fantôme	the ghost train
la grande roue	the big wheel
une entrée pour	one ticket for
taille minimum	minimum height
âge minimum	minimum age
Il faut mesurer... cm	You must be... cm tall
Il faut avoir... ans	You must be... years old
un squelette	a skeleton
une sorcière	a witch
un rire	a laugh
une chauve-souris	a bat
un hibou	an owl
un loup	a wolf
une porte	a door
des chaînes	chains
des rats	rats

Additional vocabulary for teachers

On va visiter un parc d'attractions	We are going to visit a theme park
les attractions	(f) the (theme park) rides
mon attraction préférée	(f) my favourite ride
Ça fait... euros	That comes to... euros

Resources

Pictures of and information about theme parks here and in French-speaking countries

Lesson 1 Les attractions (The rides)

Resources

Pictures of theme-park rides; individual copies of photocopiable 23A; a computer and Internet access

- Introduce the subject of theme parks. Ask the children to name, in English, some traditional theme park rides.

- Show pictures, and sketch and list four rides on the whiteboard: *le grand huit*; *le carrousel, le train fantôme, la grande roué*. Encourage actions and vary your voice (quiet to loud, sad to happy), the children repeating the names in the same way.

- Beside each ride's name, write a price: for example, *5,50* (cinq euros cinquante).

- Ask questions about the prices: for example, *La grande roué, c'est combien?*

- Suggest the children write a secret price list for the rides on their individual whiteboard. Partners ask the prices of rides, writing down the answers they hear. When they reveal their answers to each other, do they match the prices?

- Return to your price list on the whiteboard. Add further writing to the prices with an age or height restriction. For example: *Il faut mesurer 1m 20. Il faut avoir huit ans.* (You must be 1m 20 tall. You must be eight years old.)

- Ask the children to put numbers 1-4 on their individual whiteboard. In random order, read the four descriptions of prices and restrictions. Through careful listening, can the children write the correct ride's name next to its number on their whiteboard?

- Share experiences of theme parks. Which have the children visited? Have they been to any in French-speaking countries? Mention *le Parc Asterix*, a theme park only 30km north of Paris. Investigate its website on www.parcasterix.fr

- Suggest that the children in groups of four could design their own theme park. Display and translate a copy of the planning sheet, photocopiable 23A. (How much is a ticket? How much for a family? Which rides? Minimum height? Minimum age? Opening times? How many cafés and restaurants? The park's name?)

Follow-up

Display useful reference material: ride names; a copy of the planning sheet with English translations; your model answers. Encourage group discussion as the children complete their own planning sheets for a theme park. Suggest choosing the park's name later- perhaps after researching names of French cartoon characters. Listen to feedback from each group. Save the plans.

Lesson 2 C'était merveilleux! (It was marvellous!)

Resources

Pictures of theme-park rides; a computer and internet access; completed copies of photocopiable 23A (from **Follow-up**, Lesson 1)

- Speaking in the past tense, tell the children about your previous weekend: *Le weekend dernier, je suis allé(e) au parc d'attractions. C'était merveilleux! Il y avait une grande roue: c'était énorme! Il y avait aussi un train fantôme: c'était rapide et terrifiant! Mon attraction préférée était le carrousel. C'était assez lent!* (Last weekend, I went to the theme park. It was marvellous! There was a big wheel: it was enormous! There was also a ghost train: it was fast and terrifying! My favourite ride was the merry-go-round. It was quite slow!).

- Repeat your oral description. Emphasise the verbs. Explain *je suis allé(e)*. Ask about *Il y avait* and *c'était*. What do they mean? What tense are they? (Past)

- Put the children into groups of four for the memory game **Carriages**, but have a class practice first. The first person says *Je suis allé(e) au parc d'attractions et il y avait...un grand huit*. The second person in the group repeats the sentence and adds a theme park ride (a 'carriage'). The next child repeats the extended sentence and adds a third ride. The fourth child has to remember and say everything and add a ride.

- Make sketches of the four rides from Lesson 1. Ask the children to identify them.

- Without speaking, write these adjectives on the whiteboard: *merveilleux, énorme, rapide, terrifiant, fantastique, marrant, génial, sensationnel.*

- Put the children into pairs of television newsreaders. Their pronunciation matters! Can they offer each other strategies for pronouncing the words correctly?

- Share pronunciation tips: splitting words into syllables; identifying familiar graphemes; thinking of familiar words with the same ending.

Un, deux, trois!

- Read the words together. Can the children think of other appropriate adjectives to describe the rides? (*passionnant, superbe, magnifique, super*).

- Tell the children your favourite weekend ride. *Mon attraction préférée était le carrousel parce que c'était lent.* Suggest they think of their last visit to a theme park and tell a partner what their favourite ride was, using the same sentence construction. Invite individuals to tell the class.

- Make another virtual visit to *le Parc Asterix* (www.parcasterix.fr) and investigate more of the rides and entertainment. What do the children most like the look of?

Follow-up

Re-form the planning groups (**Follow-up** Lesson 1). Let groups refresh their memories and decide how to share the work: for example, one child makes and writes about just one ride.

Lesson 3 Le train fantôme (The ghost train)

Resources
Picture of a ghost train ride

- Put the children into pairs and display a picture of a ghost train ride.

- Ask the children to imagine being on this ride in a dark tunnel. Using a bilingual dictionary, let partners list three or four things they might see or hear.

- Write some on the whiteboard: *des chaînes* (chains); *un hibou* (an owl); *un rire* (a laugh); *une chauve-souris* (a bat); *une sorcière* (a witch); *un loup* (a wolf).

- Agree on a mime for each and practise the vocabulary: you say the noun and the children mime; you mime and the children say the noun.

- Tell the children they are ghost train passengers. Suggest they close their eyes. The scary ride is about to start!

- Speak this commentary, the children reacting with their faces and body language:
  – *Il fait nuit. Le train fantôme commence à rouler. Sshh. Qu'est-ce que c'est? C'est une chauve-souris? C'est terrifiant! Écoutez! Qu'est-ce que c'est? C'est un loup? Oui, c'est un loup énorme. Ecoutez! Qu'est-ce que c'est? C'est un rire horrible ! C'est la sorcière mysterieuse. Elle arrive!*
  (It's dark. The ghost train is starting to move off. Sshh. What's that?
  Is it a bat? It's terrifying! Listen! What's that? Is it a

wolf? Yes, it's an enormous wolf. Listen! What's that? It's a horrible laugh. It's the mysterious witch. She's coming!)

- Explain your commentary and choose children to act as the chorus, responsible for the sound effects. Give them name cards so they can plan what noise to make.

- Warn the class to close their eyes again as the train ride re-starts. Speak your commentary, indicating to members of the chorus when to make their sounds. Heighten the atmosphere by playing appropriate music: *Danse macabre* (Camille Saint-Saens) would be very appropriate.

- Introduce the phrases *J'ai pris, J'ai vu, J'ai entendu*. Explain that they are past tense verbs and model their use: for example, *J'ai pris le train fantôme. J'ai vu une sorcière. J'ai entendu des chaînes.* (I went for a ride on the ghost train. I saw a witch. I heard chains.)

Follow-up

Let the children tell a partner what they heard or saw when they were on a ghost train (a true or fictional account). Ask them to use your model to write about and illustrate a ghost train trip they made. Leave a bank of vocabulary on display.

Let the groups (**Follow-up** Lesson 1) continue creating their theme parks.

Lesson 4 Le weekend dernier... (Last weekend ...)

Resources
Pictures of theme-parks; individual copies of photocopiable 23B

- Keep this text unseen by the children as you read it aloud:
  Le weekend dernier, je suis allé(e) au parc d'attractions. C'était merveilleux! Il y avait une grande roue. C'était énorme! Il y avait aussi un train fantôme. C'était rapide et terrifiant! J'ai vu une sorcière. J'ai entendu des chaînes. Mon attraction préférée était le carrousel. C'était assez lent !

- Put the children into pairs with a copy of photocopiable 23B. Ask them to cut the page into its nine separate sentences and order them.

- Suggest partners read their ordered text to each other. Which version makes most sense? What does the text mean?

- Display and order the text on the whiteboard. (You could drag and drop text on an interactive whiteboard.) Enlist the children's help, identifying words and phrases that show the text is about the past. (*Le weekend dernier; je suis allé(e); C'était; Il y avait; J'ai vu*).

● Explain that this is the postcard you are sending home about your trip.

● Remove most of the text from the whiteboard, but retain its opening and important starters.
For example:
Le weekend dernier, je suis allé(e) au parc d'attractions.
C'était...
Il y avait...
J'ai entendu...
Mon attraction préférée était...

● Use this writing frame to model write a different postcard. Afterwards leave just the opening and starters on the whiteboard.

● Let the children, in pairs, write a postcard about their visit to a theme park. Make sure there is a bank of helpful vocabulary on display.

Follow-up
Suggest partners 'post' their card to another pair of children. Do the readers understand it?

Let the groups from Lesson 1 complete their theme parks and rehearse their presentation to the class.

Le Parc Asterix is a very popular theme park – partly because it is named after the well-known cartoon character Asterix. It is quite near Paris (30 km north.)

Un, deux, trois!

Un parc d'attractions

1. Combien pour une entrée?

2. Combien pour une famille?

3. Quelles attractions?

4. Taille minimum?

5. Age minimum?

6. Horaires?

7. Combien de cafés et de restaurants?

8. Le nom du parc?

Je suis allé(e) au parc d'attractions.

C'était merveilleux!

C'était énorme!

Mon attraction préférée était le carrousel.

J'ai vu une sorcière et j'ai entendu des chaînes.

Il y avait aussi un train fantôme.

Il y avait une grande roue.

C'était assez lent!

Le weekend dernier, je suis allé(e) au parc d'attractions.

C'était rapide et terrifiant!

More ideas for...

Work at school

- Make the group work from **Follow-up** Lesson 1b – an on-going task for this unit. Encourage groups to think of innovative ways to display and advertise their theme parks. Let them research French books for popular cartoon or fiction characters. These could inspire names for the theme parks and their rides.

- Give the children this simple script for buying tickets for a ride. Playing the scene in pairs, one child could be the ticket-seller, one the customer:
  A: *Une entrée pour le grand huit, s'il vous plait.*
  (A ticket for the rollercoaster, please.)

  B: *Oui, ça fait neuf euros.* (Yes, that's nine euros.)

  A: *Merci.*　　　(Thank you.)

  Encourage the children to improvise by changing the price, the ride and the number of tickets.

- Create a class display of the postcards made in Lesson 4. Explain that verbs that use *être* to form the perfect tense (for example *aller*) sometimes change the spelling of their past participle to show feminine agreement (for example *allée*). So a postcard from a girl must say *Je suis allée;* one from a boy, *Je suis allé.*

Work at home

- Give the children a list of some of the adjectives used: *passionnant; génial; terrifiant; rapide; sensationnel; marrant* and their meanings. Ask the children to learn their meanings and spellings. Suggest this will be easier if they create calligrams (the words are drawn in a way that represents their meaning – for example, the letters in *rapide* could all have roller skates on.)

- Ask the children to check their information about euros. Can they convert them into sterling? Suggest they make a dual currency price list for four rides at their theme park: in euros and sterling.

- Suggest the children see what they can find out about age restrictions at a theme park in this country. How do they compare with ones in France? Are there many rides they would be too young for?

You must visit Disneyland Paris! It's the only Disney theme park in Europe and is very similar to the American parks. Your favourite Disney characters are there!

Unit 24
Quoi de neuf passé ?

(What's in the news?)

Unit theme
- The news

Teaching points
- Making statements about newspaper columns
- Expressing and justifying opinions (using the word *car*)

Grammar
- Using the possessive adjective: *son*
- Replying to questions with *Pourquoi?*

Language sounds
- Phoneme-grapheme correspondence

Vocabulary

la rubrique météo	the weather column
la rubrique mode	the fashion column
la rubrique cuisine	the cookery column
la rubrique actualités	the current events column
la rubrique sport	the sports column
C'est intéressant/ beau/trop long	It is interesting/beautiful /too long
car	as/since
à mon/son avis	in my/his/her opinion

Additional vocabulary for teachers

le journal / les journaux	the newspaper/newspapers
un sondage	a survey
pourquoi?	why?

Resources
Jacques, the class puppet

Lesson 1 C'est intéressant (It is interesting)

Resources
A French newspaper or access to a French online newspaper; individual copies of photocopiable 24A

- Hold group and then class discussions in English about news. Pose discussion questions: What is 'news'? How do you find it out? Are newspapers useful?

- Explain that newspapers are divided into sections and columns: for example, weather.

- Put the children into pairs. Give them a copy of photocopiable 24A. Explain that the pictures represent the five columns listed. Can the children label them? Encourage partner discussion about strategies for working out meanings. What about pronunciation? Do they know words with the same ending or a familiar grapheme?

- Share pronunciation and meaning strategies before you show answers on the whiteboard and say the column names for the children to repeat.

- Show the children a paper or online French newspaper from www.onlinenewspapers.com/france Can they find *la rubrique météo, la rubrique mode, la rubrique cuisine, la rubrique actualités,* and *la rubrique sport*. Can they identify others? How?

- Without reading them aloud, write these six phrases on the whiteboard: *C'est génial / intéressant / ennuyeux / fantastique / beau / trop long* (It's brilliant / interesting / boring / fantastic / beautiful / too long).

- Put the children into groups of four, each child with a piece of card. Ask the children to write a phrase from the whiteboard, each group member choosing a different one.

- Suggest the groups use dictionaries and sort their cards into positive and negative comments. Encourage breaking words into segments and using their experience of phoneme–grapheme correspondence to work out pronunciation.

- Let the groups compare their sorting results with another group. Do they agree? Share answers as a class. Do the children know any other words for expressing an opinion?

- Are any phrases from the whiteboard still unplaced? Which type are they?

Follow-up

Opinion Bingo Call out a phrase. If groups own it, they wave it in the air and set it aside. The first group to set aside all their phrases calls 'House!'

Up/down Say an opinion phrase in a positive or negative way. If your manner of speaking matches the phrase's meaning, the children should give a thumbs up. If your voice does not match, they give a thumbs down. (For example, *C'est fantastique* said in a negative way gets a thumbs down.) Owners of the wrong thumbs are out!

Lesson 2 À mon avis (In my opinion)

Resources
The class puppet

- Return to the newspaper columns from Lesson 1. Play **Pictogram**: call out a column's name for the children to draw an appropriate picture on their individual whiteboard.

- Display these five column names: *la rubrique météo, la rubrique mode, la rubrique cuisine, la rubrique actualités, la rubrique sport.*

- Put the children into pairs or small groups. Give out copies of photocopiable 24B.

- Allow reading time. Encourage identifying familiar words to gain a gist of what the text is about. Are some other meanings easily guessed? (*contagieux, domicile*).

- Ask the children general questions, in English, about the content.

- Point to the column headings. Where should this article go? (*la rubrique actualités*).

- Write two sentences on the whiteboard: *J'aime la rubrique sport. Le sport est intéressant.* Ask about

the meaning. (I like the sports column. Sport is interesting.)

- Let the children use the same two-sentence pattern to tell their partner:
  1. which column they like/dislike;
  2. why they like/dislike it.

- Listen to some of the children's sentences.

- Return to your two sentences on the whiteboard. Suggest linking them into one sentence. What connective do the children know? (*parce que*) What other ones do they know in English? (for, as).

- Introduce the phrase *car à mon avis* (for in my opinion). Demonstrate its use: *J'aime la rubrique actualités car à mon avis c'est intéressant.*

- Get out Jacques, your class puppet. Ask *Tu aimes la rubrique mode?* Let him answer *Non, je n'aime pas la rubrique mode car à mon avis c'est ridicule.* (Do you like the fashion column? No, I don't like the fashion column as in my opinion it's ridiculous.) Give the children oral practice in using the connective phrase.

- Ask the children to choose and write down:
  - three newspaper columns;
  - three questions to ask people about liking those columns – for example, *Tu aimes la rubrique sport?*

Follow-up
Let the children conduct and save a newspaper survey, asking four children a question. Suggest they draw and write the person's name and record their answer in a speech bubble. (For example: *Non, je n'aime pas la rubrique mode car à mon avis la mode est ridicule.*)

Lesson 3 À son avis (In his/her opinion)

Resources
A computer and large display screen (preferably an interactive whiteboard); the children's surveys from **Follow-up** Lesson 2

- Put the children into small groups and set a timed challenge: to write down the names of the five newspaper columns. (If necessary, provide visual clues or initial letters.)

- Return the surveys done in **Follow-up** Lesson 2. Display part of your own survey:
  - a question: *Tu aimes la rubrique mode?* and a picture of Jacques;
  - a speech bubble containing his answer: *Non, je n'aime pas la rubrique mode car à mon avis c'est ridicule.*

- Point out the possessive adjective *mon*? What does it mean? (my) Ask the children to find *mon* in the answers they were given.

- Remove your display, explaining that you prefer to tell them about Jacques. Say and write *Jacques n'aime pas la rubrique mode car à son avis c'est ridicule.*

- Do the children spot a change? Why has *mon* become *son*? (*son* is the third person possessive adjective meaning his or her). Give the children another example sentence.

- Put the children into small groups. Using their surveys from **Follow-up**, Lesson 2, but not displaying them, they should report to one another some children's opinions. Encourage them to help one another to use *son* instead of *mon*. Let some children report to the class.

- Now tell the children your exciting idea: a newspaper in which the children will write about themselves – their likes, dislikes and plans for the future.

- Form writing groups of about four children to plan and write an introductory paragraph. This will form the first page of the newspaper. Ask them to write: that it is the end of the school year; that the class is leaving; the name of the class; where they will be going in September; what this newspaper is about.

- Display some helpful phrases, perhaps from the example text below.

Follow-up
Share results. Work as a class, forming, improving and ordering sentences. Use a computer, with the agreed text displayed on an interactive whiteboard.
For example:

Salut! C'est juillet et c'est la fin de l'année scolaire. La classe, qui s'appelle le EJ6, va quitter l'école! En septembre les enfants vont à l'école secondaire. Dans notre journal d'école, vous pouvez tout apprendre sur les enfants.

(Hello! It's July and the end of the school year. Class EJ6 is leaving the school! In September the children are going to secondary school. In our school newspaper, you can find out all about the children.)
Save your text.

Le Figaro and Le Monde are France's two most famous newspapers.

Lesson 4 Notre journal d'école (Our school newspaper)

Resources
Individual copies of the planning questionnaire shown; individual access to computers

- Remind the children about their class newspaper and the introduction (**Follow-up** Lesson 4). They now have to write their personal articles.

- Give everyone this planning questionnaire to write answers:
  Comment tu t'appelles? (What are you called?)
  Quel âge as-tu? (How old are you?)
  As-tu un frère ou une soeur? (Do you have a brother or sister?)
  Tu aimes la musique? (Do you like music?)
  Où habites-tu? (Where do you live?)
  Tu joues le football? (Do you play football?)

- Display Jacques' written answers: *Je m'appelle Jacques. J'ai dix ans. J'ai une soeur. J'aime la musique. J'habite à Londres. Oui, je joue le football.*

- Demonstrate how Jacques uses his planning answers to help him create a text:
  – *Bonjour! Je m'appelle Jacques. J'ai dix ans. J'ai une soeur qui a huit ans. J'aime beaucoup la musique pop car à mon avis c'est fantastique. J'habite à Londres. Je joue le football et le golf. Je voudrais devenir golfeur.*

- Point out that Jacques has sometimes added detail to his original answers. Highlight and explain the last sentence. (I would like to become a golfer) Ask everyone to add this *Je voudrais devenir… (instituteur)* (…a teacher) to their planning sheet.

- Suggest they write the final word on their individual whiteboard and draw a picture. Holding the boards up, the children should group themselves into newspaper columns.

- Agree on the columns' names and list them under your newspaper's introduction.

Follow-up
Suggest the children write a draft version of their article for a partner to check, and then write or type the final version. An illustration – paper or electronic – will add interesting detail.

Collate the articles into both paper and electronic newspapers: visitors to the school will enjoy reading it in the entrance hall; users of the school's website will be delighted to find an online copy.

Un journal

la rubrique cuisine

la rubrique actualités

la rubrique météo

la rubrique sport

la rubrique mode

C'est le Swine Flu

Le virus est contagieux plus de cinq jours

Il y a une maladie terrible en France. C'est le Swine Flu. Beaucoup d'élèves dans deux écoles à Paris sont très malades. Trois enfants sont à l'hôpital. Ils sont infectés par le virus H1N1. Ce virus s'appelle le Swine Flu. Un garçon a visité Mexico et il était malade. Quand il a retourné à Paris, il était contagieux. Maintenant, son école et l'école de sa sœur ferment les portes durant une semaine. Tous les élèves restent à leur domicile.

- -

Translation:

Virus contagious for more than five days

There is a terrible illness in France. It's Swine Flu. Many pupils in two schools in Paris are very ill. Three children are in hospital. They are infected by the virus H1N1. The virus is called swine flu. One boy visited Mexico and was ill. When he returned to Paris, he was contagious. Now, his school and his sister's school are closed for a week. All the pupils are staying at home.

More ideas for...

Work at school

- Ask the children to list the adjectives in photocopiable 23B, Part 1 and to write their masculine and plural forms. Can they find examples of the third person singular possessive adjective in this text? (*son, sa*)

- Commission the children, in pairs or small groups, to write an article about a new theme park or café in their town. Refresh their memories with a bank of useful vocabulary from Units 21 and 23.

- Make a display of the class's likes and dislikes. One half of the board can be headed **J'aime...** the other half headed **Je n'aime pas...** Let the children draw self-portraits and speech bubbles with information about their likes or dislikes.

- Give the children opportunities to look at online French newspapers. Can they understand the headlines? What interesting news do they manage to find out?

- Play oral games with **Pourquoi**? (Why?) Let the children make statements expressing opinions. Encourage them to justify their opinions with *À mon avis...* or *parce que...*

Work at home

- Give the children a copy of photocopiable 23B, Part 1. Ask them to answer these comprehension questions in English. How good are their translation skills?
  Questions:
  1. What is the article about?
  2. Which section of the paper would you put it in?
  3. What is the name of the illness?
  4. How many schools are involved?
  5. Where are the schools?
  6. How many children are in hospital?
  7. Who started the illness in the schools?
  8. How long are the two schools closed?

- Suggest the children read part of a newspaper every day for a week. Encourage them to read articles from different columns in the paper. At the end of the week, what do they have to report? In school, let them express opinions about what they read, reporting to a partner or small group.

- Give the children a copy of the planning questionnaire used in Lesson 4. Ask the children to interview a family member and record their answers. Back at school, let them report some of the answers given speaking in the third person: for example: *Il aime le sport.*

The main French newspapers are in paper form and also online.

Un, deux, trois!

Other books in the series

Un, deux, trois! - Lower Juniors
Years 3-4

Hopscotch

A division of MA Education Ltd

Published by
Hopscotch, a division of MA Education,
St Jude's Church, Dulwich Road,
London, SE24 0PB
www.hopscotchbooks.com
020 7738 5454

Notes

Notes

Notes

Notes

Notes